Best of the Best

the best recipes from the 25 best cookbooks of the year

from the editors of

FOOD&**WINE**

FOOD & WINE BEST OF THE BEST VOL. 11
EDITOR **Kate Heddings**
ART DIRECTOR **Patricia Sanchez**
DESIGNER **James Maikowski**
SENIOR EDITOR **Zoe Singer**
ASSOCIATE FOOD EDITOR **Melissa Rubel**
COPY EDITOR **Lisa Leventer**
PRODUCTION MANAGER **Matt Carson**
REPORTERS **Kristin Donnelly, Emily McKenna, Melissa Rubel, Kelly Snowden, Emery Van Hook**

COVER
PHOTOGRAPH Tina Rupp
FOOD STYLING Jamie Kimm
PROP STYLING Alistair Turnbull

FLAP PHOTOGRAPHS
DANA COWIN PORTRAIT Andrew French
KATE HEDDINGS PORTRAIT Andrew French

FOOD & WINE MAGAZINE
EDITOR IN CHIEF **Dana Cowin**
CREATIVE DIRECTOR **Stephen Scoble**
MANAGING EDITOR **Mary Ellen Ward**
EXECUTIVE EDITOR **Pamela Kaufman**
EXECUTIVE FOOD EDITOR **Tina Ujlaki**
ART DIRECTOR **Patricia Sanchez**

AMERICAN EXPRESS PUBLISHING CORPORATION
PRESIDENT/C.E.O. **Ed Kelly**
S.V.P./CHIEF MARKETING OFFICER **Mark V. Stanich**
C.F.O./S.V.P./CORPORATE DEVELOPMENT
& OPERATIONS **Paul B. Francis**
V.P., BOOKS & PRODUCTS **Marshall Corey**
DIRECTOR, BOOK PROGRAMS **Bruce Spanier**
DIRECTOR, CUSTOMER RETENTION & LOYALTY **Greg D'Anca**
SENIOR MARKETING MANAGER, BRANDED BOOKS **Eric Lucie**
DIRECTOR OF FULFILLMENT **Phil Black**
MANAGER OF CUSTOMER EXPERIENCE &
PRODUCT DEVELOPMENT **Charles Graver**
BUSINESS MANAGER **Tom Noonan**
ASSOCIATE BUSINESS MANAGER **Desiree Bernardez**
PRODUCTION DIRECTOR **Rosalie Abatemarco Samat**
CORPORATE PRODUCTION MANAGER **Stuart Handelman**

ISBN 1-932624-32-5
ISSN 1524-2862

Published by American Express Publishing Corporation
1120 Avenue of the Americas, New York, New York 10036

Manufactured in the United States of America

Best of the Best

the best recipes from the 25 best cookbooks of the year

VOL. 11

FOOD&**WINE**
BOOKS

American Express Publishing Corporation, New York

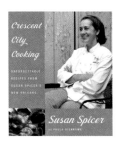

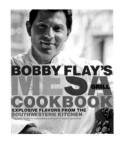

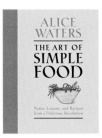

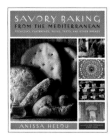

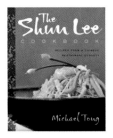

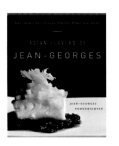

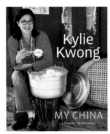

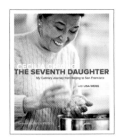

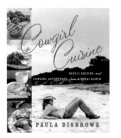

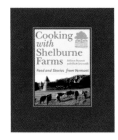

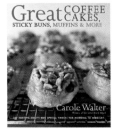

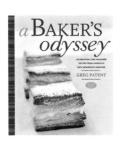

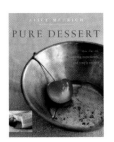

CONTENTS

best of the best exclusives Recipe titles in **bold** are brand-new dishes appearing exclusively in *Best of the Best*.

CONTENTS

best of the best exclusives Recipe titles in **bold** are brand-new dishes appearing exclusively in *Best of the Best*.

BAKING

RECIPES

Poultry

Meat

Vegetables & Sides

Desserts

FOREWORD

To put together *The Best of the Best,* we tested (and tasted) recipes from over 100 cookbooks to pick the top 25 of the year. A few trends were easy to spot. For instance, 2007 was a big year for chefs and restaurateurs to return to their roots. In one of our five chapters, "Chef Showcases," Bobby Flay pays homage to his first restaurant with the *Mesa Grill Cookbook,* pledging his allegiance to the contemporary Southwestern cuisine that made him a star. In our "Asian" chapter, Michael Tong (*The Shun Lee Cookbook*) and Cecilia Chiang (*The Seventh Daughter*) reflect on their lengthy restaurant careers and share their success stories and super-delicious recipes.

Another notable theme for '07 was getting back to basics, prompted by the movement to eat locally and pay more attention to ingredients. In *Cook with Jamie,* British chef and philanthropist Jamie Oliver strives to teach novices as well as experienced cooks how to shop mindfully and cook with confidence. And Alice Waters breaks away from her series of Chez Panisse books (eight of them in total) with *The Art of Simple Food,* a lovely book that teaches fundamental cooking techniques with easy, beautiful recipes that—not surprisingly—are best made with the freshest local ingredients.

Trends come and go, but one trait of some of our favorite cookbooks ever is that they are as compelling to read as they are to cook from. In *A Baker's Odyssey,* one of four terrific titles in our "Baking" section, Greg Patent tells how immigrants from around the world have adapted their recipes to American ingredients and kitchens. Our "Mediterranean" chapter features another great read: *Mediterranean Harvest,* in which Martha Rose Shulman delves into the history of the vegetarian recipes she discovered on her travels from Croatia to France to Lebanon.

We are thrilled to have found so many wonderful recipes from so many fantastic cookbooks. And we're especially proud of the never-before-published recipes that many of these authors have so generously shared here; they're some of the tastiest in the book!

Dana Cowin
Editor in Chief
FOOD & WINE Magazine

Editor
FOOD & WINE Cookbooks

CHEF SHOWCASES

BARBECUED CHICKEN SALAD
WITH CORN, AVOCADO & CREAMY
POBLANO DRESSING, P. 16

CRESCENT CITY COOKING

SUSAN SPICER WITH PAULA DISBROWE

PUBLISHED BY ALFRED A. KNOPF, $35

New Orleans chef Susan Spicer has a talent for creating bold, brawny flavors, as evidenced by this, her first cookbook, a compilation of greatest hits from her sensational restaurants Bayona and Herbsaint as well as favorites from her travels. "It's taken me 26 years to tackle my first cookbook," she writes. "I needed to travel and expand the range of my palate, then condense my wild, delicious ride into a selection of very personal, hand-chosen recipes—from my restaurants and my life." The result is an eclectic, appealing mix of New Orleans classics like dirty rice and crayfish pies crusted with cornmeal along with a smattering of recipes from farther afield, including a spicy Thai salad inspired by a trip to Bangkok and a layered crêpe "gâteau" from a renowned restaurant in Lyon, France.

featured recipes Barbecued Chicken Salad with Corn, Avocado & Creamy Poblano Dressing; Roasted Chicken with Olives, Lemon & Garlic; Smoked Duck & Andouille Gumbo; Wild & Dirty Rice

best of the best exclusive Bayona Snapper Ceviche with Guacamole

Find more recipes by Susan Spicer at foodandwine.com/spicer.

BARBECUED CHICKEN SALAD WITH CORN, AVOCADO & CREAMY POBLANO DRESSING

SERVES 4
PREP TIME 30 MINUTES

1½ to 2 cups diced barbecued chicken meat, from leftovers or a store-bought roasted chicken
1 ripe avocado, diced
½ cup frozen corn kernels, thawed, or 2 ears corn, grilled in the husk (see Grilling Corn), then shucked and cut from the cob
¼ cup thinly sliced celery or celery hearts
3 scallions, thinly sliced
1 head Bibb lettuce, broken into leaves, washed, and dried
Creamy Poblano Dressing (recipe follows)

I have never been able to do the cold-pizza-for-breakfast thing, but there are some foods I just love eating cold the day after—fried or barbecued chicken, for instance. Happily, my local grocery store does rotisserie chicken, either plain or barbecue, and on weeknights when homework is taking forever, I am grateful for this easy main course salad that the kids will actually dig into. For my husband and me, it's all about the creamy, spicy poblano dressing. But for the kids it's strictly ranch—no cilantro, please! For a more substantial meal, serve this with corn bread or, better yet, jalapeño corn bread (add chopped pickled jalapeños to your favorite recipe).

Toss all the ingredients except dressing in a salad bowl, then toss in the dressing or serve it on the side.

GRILLING CORN Grilled corn has a sweet, smoky flavor that's great on its own (eaten off the cob with butter and a squirt of lime) and in salads. You'll want to grill the corn in its husk, because this preserves moisture and imparts a distinctive sweet and "corny" flavor. Simply soak the ears in cold water for about 20 minutes. Place them directly on a medium-low grill or over pale gray coals, and cover. Grill for about 20 minutes, turning the cobs every 5 minutes to ensure even cooking. As with any cooked corn, you'll know it's done when the kernels are tender and release a milky liquid when pierced. Peel away the husk and silk and serve as you wish.

VARIATIONS

Feel free to also add red peppers, tomatoes, and cotija (an aged Mexican cheese) or any crumbly white cheese to the salad.

This salad is also delicious with corn bread croutons. (Day-old corn bread actually works best, because it will be drier. If you use fresh, you can dry it out in a 350°F oven for a few minutes.) Cut the corn bread into cubes, toss them with a little melted butter, and toast in a 350°F oven until golden brown and crisp. Let them cool, and toss with the salad.

Creamy Poblano Dressing

1 poblano, roasted and peeled
  (see Roasting Peppers and Chiles)
2 tablespoons fresh
  lime juice
2 tablespoons chopped
  scallion greens
1 garlic clove
1 cup mayonnaise
2 tablespoons sour cream or
  buttermilk

Taste a portion of the poblano. Some are spicier than others, so adjust the amount accordingly. If it's really spicy you might want to add more mayo.

Place all the ingredients in a blender and puree until smooth. Adjust seasonings as necessary.

EDITOR'S NOTE
This spicy dressing is thick and creamy enough to double as a dip. Set out a bowl with raw vegetables, steamed shrimp or tortilla chips.

ROASTING PEPPERS AND CHILES To roast fresh poblanos or other peppers or chiles, place them directly on the grill over a low flame on a gas range, or on a baking sheet under a broiler, and char until evenly blackened, turning as necessary. Transfer peppers to a bowl and cover with a hand towel for about 5 minutes to steam the peppers (this will make their skins easier to remove). Alternatively, you can steam the peppers in a sealed plastic bag. Use your paring knife and/or your fingers to remove the stem, seeds, and skin from the peppers and use the smoky flesh as directed in the recipe.

ROASTED CHICKEN WITH OLIVES, LEMON & GARLIC

SERVES 4
PREP TIME 1 HOUR 15 MINUTES

  1 chicken (2½ to 3 pounds)
  2 lemons, zested and quartered
12 to 15 garlic cloves, crushed and peeled
  3 tablespoons olive oil
Salt and pepper
Crushed red pepper flakes
6 to 8 sprigs rosemary (strip half the
      sprigs of their leaves and chop
      coarsely)
  1 medium onion, peeled and cut
      into 8 wedges
  1 cup pitted kalamata or picholine
      olives, or a combination of both

Think there's no way to improve upon perfectly roasted chicken? Think again. At Herbsaint we would have to appoint someone to guard the pans while these birds cooled, or they would all end up wingless! In this recipe, the addition of rosemary, garlic, lemon, and olives perfumes the meat and suggests a world of accompaniments: steamed artichokes, just-cooked angel hair pasta, fluffy couscous, a salad of pungent greens with crusty bread for sopping up the juices. When it comes to wine, consider serving a rosé or a white from the Rhone valley.

Preheat the oven to 450°F. Place a 13 x 9-inch roasting pan in the oven.

Rinse the chicken and use paper towels to pat it dry, inside and out. Squeeze 1 of the lemon quarters over the skin and rub the juice around with your fingers. Using your fingers to gently separate the skin from the breast, place a couple of the garlic cloves and some of the lemon zest under the skin of the breast on each side. Let it sit about 10 minutes, then pat the bird dry again, rub the skin with 2 tablespoons olive oil, and season with the salt, pepper, red pepper, and some of the chopped rosemary. Make an incision on the inside of each thigh and insert a garlic clove. Place 3 of the garlic cloves in the cavity, along with the rosemary sprigs and 2 of the lemon quarters.

continued on p. 20

You may tie the legs together over the cavity, if you like. Place the chicken breast side up in the preheated roasting pan. Bake for about 30 minutes, watching to make sure the chicken starts to brown. Carefully loosen the chicken from the pan with a spatula and turn it over to brown the underside.

At this point, lower the oven heat to 400°F. Add the remaining tablespoon olive oil to the pan, then scatter the onion, olives, remaining garlic, lemon quarters and zest, and chopped rosemary around the chicken and cook for about 15 minutes. Turn the chicken over again and stir the onion, olives, and garlic around a little. Cook another 10 to 15 minutes to re-crisp the skin.

When the chicken is a deep golden brown, remove it from the oven and let it sit for about 5 minutes. Transfer the chicken to a plate and collect any juices that drain. Tilt the roasting pan and spoon off the fat, if desired. Stir the olives, onion, and lemon around, pressing on the lemon a little to extract the juice. Add the chicken juices to the pan and scrape the brown bits off the bottom of the pan to incorporate them into the mixture. Spoon the juicy olive-onion mixture around the chicken and serve.

SMOKED DUCK & ANDOUILLE GUMBO

SERVES 8
PREP TIME 3 HOURS (INCLUDES
DUCK ROASTING TIME)

- 4 duck legs, or 1 whole duck
- Salt and pepper
- ½ cup vegetable oil or rendered duck fat, plus extra for cooking okra
- ½ cup flour
- 2 medium onions, chopped
- 2 bell peppers, chopped
- 3 celery stalks, chopped
- ½ pound andouille sausage, halved lengthwise and sliced
- 4 to 5 garlic cloves, minced
- 6 cups rich chicken stock (see Enriching Chicken Broth on p. 22)
- 2 cups sliced okra, fresh or frozen
- ½ cup plus 2 tablespoons chopped scallions
- 1 teaspoon chopped fresh thyme
- 1 teaspoon filé powder (see Filé Powder on p. 22), optional
- 1 tablespoon Worcestershire sauce
- Bouquet Garni (recipe follows)
- Hot sauce
- Cooked white rice, optional

EDITOR'S NOTE

Andouille, a spiced, smoked Cajun sausage, is increasingly available at specialty markets; you can also order it from cajungrocer.com. For this gumbo, kielbasa is a good replacement.

Although I was not born in New Orleans—we moved here when I was six—I most definitely consider it my hometown. Even post-hurricanes, I am eternally grateful to my dad for deciding to make this simmering, sumptuous, gumbo-of-a-city our permanent home when he retired from the navy. What a happy circumstance for a food lover like me!

Speaking of gumbo, I could eat it every day of the week. And you can't claim to be a cook in Louisiana without having your own version of its most famous dish. While I have to say that Donald Link, the chef at Herbsaint, makes the best gumbo I have ever eaten, I've learned to make a pretty mean version myself. Here is one of the most basic. Feel free to substitute an equal amount of roasted chicken for the duck.

Preheat the oven to 350°F. Place the duck in a roasting pan and season with salt and pepper. Roast the legs for about 1 hour (the whole duck for about 2 hours), until tender. If desired, save the rendered fat to make the roux. Let the duck cool and pick the meat off the bones.

Heat the ½ cup oil (or duck fat) in a large, heavy-bottomed Dutch oven or cast-iron pot over medium-high heat until almost smoking. Add the flour and whisk constantly until the roux turns a deep brown resembling the color of peanut butter (or even a little darker, for a richer flavor), 10 to 12 minutes. Add the onions, peppers, and celery, reduce the heat to medium, and cook, stirring, for 5 minutes. Stir in the sausage and cook 3 more minutes. Then add the garlic and whisk in the stock, 1 cup at a time. Bring to a boil, reduce the heat, and simmer for 15 minutes.

continued on p. 22

Heat 2 tablespoons vegetable oil in a small skillet over medium-high heat. When the oil is hot but not smoking, sear the okra and add to the pot, along with ½ cup scallions. Add the thyme, optional filé powder, Worcestershire sauce, Bouquet Garni, hot sauce to taste, the reserved duck meat, and a little salt. Simmer over low heat, stirring from time to time, for at least 1 hour. Skim off any fat from the top. Season with salt, pepper, and hot sauce and serve hot, with or without rice. Garnish with the reserved scallions.

ENRICHING CHICKEN BROTH To enrich your chicken broth or intensify a store-bought one, pour it into a pot, add the picked duck or chicken bones, and simmer for 15 minutes. You may need to add a little water to make sure you end up with 6 cups.

FILÉ POWDER An essential ingredient in Creole cooking, filé powder is a spice made from cured sassafras leaves. The Choctaw Indians from the southern Louisiana bayou taught the Cajuns to use the spice, which has an earthy, woodsy flavor.

Bouquet Garni

Having trained with French chefs, I find a bouquet garni— a pretty little bundle of fresh herbs—an indispensable seasoning for adding depth and an herbaceous perfume to stocks, soups, and sauces. Plus I always feel just a little more French when I cinch one up.

To assemble one, take 1 bunch of parsley stems, stripped of leaves (or most of them), 2 small bay leaves or 1 medium,

BOUQUET GARNI

and a generous sprig of fresh thyme. Lay the parsley stems down and spread them a little, then place the bay leaf and thyme in the center and surround with the parsley stems. Cut a 15-inch piece of kitchen twine and pick up the bundle in your left hand. Holding the string about 3 inches from the end between the thumb and index finger of your left hand, use your right hand to wrap the string twice around one end of the bundle, then bring the string down to the other end, wrapping around twice, then back to the middle and around once, meeting the 3-inch piece and tying a secure knot. Some folks like to leave a long piece to tie the bouquet onto the pot handle (making it easier to remove later), but I usually just trim it short. In a nod to French perfectionism, I also trim the ends of the herbs so they're nice and neat. And be sure to tie it snugly. If the bundle is not tied tightly, it can disintegrate when the parsley stems cook and become limp.

WILD & DIRTY RICE

SERVES 6 TO 8
PREP TIME 35 MINUTES

- 1 **cup wild rice**
- ½ **pound ground pork**
- 2 **tablespoons butter, oil, or bacon fat**
- 1 **small onion, diced**
- 2 **celery stalks, finely chopped**
- 1 **small green bell pepper, finely chopped**
- ½ **red bell pepper, finely chopped**
- 2 **garlic cloves, minced**
- ½ **pound chicken or duck livers, trimmed and coarsely chopped**
- 1 **cup long-grain white rice**
- 1½ **cups chicken stock**
- 1 **teaspoon Worcestershire sauce**
- 1 **teaspoon chopped fresh thyme**
- 1 **tablespooon chopped fresh parsley**
- 1 **small bay leaf**

Salt and pepper
Hot sauce

- ½ **bunch scallions, finely chopped (about ¼ cup)**

Plain ole dirty rice is a good thing. Add the earthy, nutty taste and toothsome texture of wild rice, and you have something even better.

Bring a 2-quart saucepan of water to boil over medium-high heat. Add the wild rice, reduce the heat, and simmer covered for 30 to 40 minutes, until the grains are tender and the ends have just slightly popped. Drain the rice in a colander and set aside.

While the rice is cooking, cook the ground pork in a medium skillet over medium heat, stirring to break up any clumps, until it is no longer pink, about 5 minutes. Drain the excess fat and set aside.

Melt the butter in a wide, shallow skillet or Dutch oven over medium-high heat. Add the onion, celery, green and red peppers, and garlic, and cook, stirring, until softened, 5 to 7 minutes. Add the livers and cooked pork and cook, stirring, until the livers are browned. Stir in the white rice, chicken stock, Worcestershire sauce, thyme, parsley, bay leaf, and ½ teaspoon salt and bring to a boil. Cover and cook over low heat about 15 minutes, until the rice is tender. Stir in the wild rice and cook for 5 more minutes. Remove from the heat and let sit, covered, for an additional 5 minutes. To serve, remove the bay leaf, season with salt, pepper, and hot sauce, and stir in the chopped scallions.

NOTE When cooking rice, I find that covering the surface of the water with a piece of waxed paper or parchment paper cut to fit the shape of the pot helps keep the rice moist and makes it cook more evenly. For more moisture and a richer flavor, stir in a cup of diced sautéed or roasted eggplant when you add the stock.

best of the best exclusive

BAYONA SNAPPER CEVICHE WITH GUACAMOLE

SERVES 4

- 1 pound skinless red snapper fillets, cut into ¼-inch dice
- ½ small red onion, finely diced
- 1 large jalapeño, seeded and minced
- ½ cup plus 3 tablespoons fresh lime juice (from 4 limes)
- Kosher salt
- 2 Hass avocados, cut into ½-inch dice
- 1 scallion, thinly sliced
- 1 small garlic clove, minced
- 1 teaspoon hot sauce
- Tortilla chips, for serving

EDITOR'S NOTE
Spicer serves this excellent ceviche at Bayona, her flagship New Orleans restaurant. She sometimes likes to use grouper or redfish (a.k.a. red drum) in place of the snapper.

1. In a medium bowl, mix the snapper with the onion, jalapeño, ½ cup plus 2 tablespoons of the lime juice and 1½ teaspoons of kosher salt. Cover and refrigerate the ceviche for 30 minutes.

2. In a medium bowl, gently mix the avocado with the scallion, garlic, hot sauce and the remaining 1 tablespoon of lime juice; season the guacamole with salt.

3. Using a slotted spoon, transfer the ceviche to bowls. Top with the guacamole and serve with tortilla chips, for scooping.

MUSSELS IN RED CHILE
PESTO BROTH, P. 28

BOBBY FLAY'S MESA GRILL COOKBOOK

BOBBY FLAY WITH STEPHANIE BANYAS & SALLY JACKSON

PUBLISHED BY CLARKSON POTTER, $35

Chef Bobby Flay has four regular TV gigs, four restaurants and seven cookbooks; what started it all was the opening in 1991 of the breakthrough Mesa Grill, a Manhattan restaurant that created a stir with its modern Southwestern cooking. Now, finally, Flay has published the *Mesa Grill Cookbook,* with bold-flavored dishes featuring ingredients like chiles, green onions, beans, corn, avocado and tomatillos. The sophistication of the recipes is impressive, but what shines through in this book is Flay's loyalty to the unbelievably delicious food of the Southwest that made him a star. As Flay writes, "The temptation to integrate the hot and trendy ingredients or cuisines of the moment has been fended off by an allegiance to a cuisine that has helped shape my career."

featured recipes Mussels in Red Chile Pesto Broth; Sweet Potato Gratin; Frisée Salad with Chorizo & Roasted Garlic Vinaigrette

best of the best exclusive Apple Salad with Walnuts, Blue Cheese & Pomegranate Vinaigrette

Find more recipes by Bobby Flay at foodandwine.com/flay.

BOBBY FLAY'S
MESA GRILL
COOKBOOK

BOBBY FLAY WITH
STEPHANIE BANYAS
& SALLY JACKSON

MUSSELS IN RED CHILE PESTO BROTH

SERVES 4

    2   ancho chiles, soaked
    2   New Mexico red chiles, soaked
    ¼   cup plus 2 tablespoons chopped
        fresh cilantro
    3   cloves garlic, chopped
    2   tablespoons pine nuts
    ½   cup extra-virgin olive oil
Kosher salt and freshly ground
        black pepper
    2   cups dry white wine
    2   pounds cultivated mussels,
        scrubbed
    2   teaspoons honey
Fresh cilantro leaves, for garnish
        (optional)

EDITOR'S NOTE

To soak dried chiles, place them in a heatproof bowl and cover with boiling water. Let the chiles stand until they are soft and pliable (typically 20 to 30 minutes).

Mussels take no time at all to cook and this red chile pesto comes together quickly as well. This fast and easy dish becomes a full meal with the addition of a salad and some bread to soak up the fruity, spicy, briny red chile–mussel sauce.

1. Remove both kinds of chiles from their soaking liquid, reserving the liquid, and seed and coarsely chop. Put the chiles in the bowl of a food processor along with ¼ cup of the soaking liquid, the ¼ cup cilantro, the garlic, and pine nuts and process until smooth. With the motor running, slowly add the oil and process until emulsified; season with salt and pepper. This can be made 1 day in advance and stored in the refrigerator.

2. Bring the wine to a boil in a large pot over high heat. Add the mussels, and cover and steam until opened, 3 to 5 minutes, discarding any that do not open. Transfer the mussels to 4 large bowls with a slotted spoon.

3. Return the cooking liquid to a boil and let reduce by half, 8 to 10 minutes. Whisk in the red chile pesto and honey. Season with salt and pepper to taste and stir in the 2 tablespoons cilantro. Pour the mixture over the mussels and serve immediately, topped with cilantro leaves, if desired.

BOBBY FLAY'S
MESA GRILL
COOKBOOK

BOBBY FLAY WITH
STEPHANIE BANYAS
& SALLY JACKSON

SWEET POTATO GRATIN

SERVES 4 TO 6

2 cups heavy cream
1 tablespoon chipotle chile puree
4 medium sweet potatoes, peeled
   and sliced ⅛ inch thick
Kosher salt and freshly ground
   black pepper
Thinly sliced green onion, white and
   green parts, for garnish (optional)

EDITOR'S NOTE

Chipotle chile puree is easy
to make—just pulse a can of
chipotles in adobo sauce in
a food processor until smooth.
Leftovers can be refrigerated
in a tightly covered container
for 1 month.

*This decadent gratin could become your next holiday
classic. The slightly spicy and smoky chipotle puree
provides a great balance to the sweet potatoes and cream
and takes this dish to another level of flavor. It's amazing
how good three ingredients can be.*

1. Preheat the oven to 375°F.

2. Whisk together the cream and chipotle puree.

3. In a 10-inch square baking dish with 2-inch-high sides,
arrange an even layer of potatoes on the bottom of the
dish, drizzle with 3 tablespoons of the cream mixture, and
season with salt and pepper. Repeat with the remaining
potatoes, cream, and salt and pepper to form 9 to 10 layers.
Press down on the gratin to totally submerge the potatoes
in the cream mixture.

4. Cover with aluminum foil and bake for 30 minutes.
Uncover and continue baking for 30 to 45 minutes, until the
cream has been absorbed, the potatoes are cooked through,
and the top is browned.

5. Remove from the oven and let rest for 10 minutes
before slicing. Top with green onion. This can be made up
to 1 day ahead and refrigerated. Reheat before serving.

BOBBY FLAY'S
MESA GRILL
COOKBOOK

BOBBY FLAY WITH
STEPHANIE BANYAS
& SALLY JACKSON

FRISÉE SALAD WITH CHORIZO & ROASTED GARLIC VINAIGRETTE

SERVES 4

- 1 tablespoon olive oil
- 12 ounces Spanish chorizo sausage, sliced ¼ inch thick
- 8 ounces frisée, torn into bite-sized pieces
- Roasted Garlic Vinaigrette
- Kosher salt and freshly ground black pepper
- 3 plum tomatoes, quartered
- Thinly shaved Asiago cheese or Parmigiano-Reggiano, for garnish
- Chopped fresh cilantro, for garnish (optional)

EDITOR'S NOTE

To roast garlic, place unpeeled cloves on a piece of foil, drizzle with olive oil and fold the foil to create a packet. Roast at 350°F until the cloves are soft and golden, about 40 minutes. Let the cloves cool, then peel them.

MAKES ABOUT 1 CUP

- 8 cloves roasted garlic, peeled
- 3 tablespoons red wine vinegar
- 1 tablespoon chopped red onion
- 1 tablespoon honey
- 1 tablespoon fresh lime juice
- Kosher salt and freshly ground black pepper
- ½ cup olive oil

The French have their frisée aux lardons; *Mesa Grill has this salad, where spicy chorizo replaces the bacon, and shaved Asiago cheese trumps the standard poached egg. This may look like a lot of garlic, but roasting it makes it sweet, not overwhelming.*

1. Heat the oil in a large skillet over high heat. Add the sausage and cook until lightly browned on both sides, 4 to 5 minutes. Remove with a slotted spoon to a plate lined with paper towels.

2. Place the frisée in a large bowl, add ¼ cup of the vinaigrette, season with salt and pepper, and toss to coat. Place the tomatoes in a bowl, add a few tablespoons of the dressing, season with salt and pepper, and toss to coat.

3. Divide the frisée among 4 large plates, arrange 3 of the tomato quarters and 5 slices of the chorizo around the perimeter of each plate. Garnish with shaved cheese and chopped cilantro and drizzle with the remaining vinaigrette.

Roasted Garlic Vinaigrette

Combine the garlic, vinegar, onion, honey, lime juice, and salt and pepper to taste in a blender and blend until smooth. With the motor running, slowly add the oil and blend until emulsified. This can be made up to 1 day ahead and refrigerated.

BOBBY FLAY'S
MESA GRILL
COOKBOOK

BOBBY FLAY WITH
STEPHANIE BANYAS
& SALLY JACKSON

best of the best exclusive

APPLE SALAD WITH WALNUTS, BLUE CHEESE & POMEGRANATE VINAIGRETTE

SERVES 6

- 1 cup walnut halves
- 1½ tablespoons pomegranate molasses
- 1 tablespoon red wine vinegar
- 2 teaspoons Dijon mustard
- 1½ teaspoons honey
- ¼ cup extra-virgin olive oil
- Kosher salt and freshly ground pepper
- 4 Granny Smith apples (2 pounds)— halved, cored and cut into ½-inch dice
- 2 cups baby spinach
- 2 Belgian endives, sliced crosswise ¼ inch thick
- 5 ounces Maytag blue cheese, crumbled

1. Preheat the oven to 350°F. Spread the walnuts in a pie plate and toast in the oven for 8 minutes, until golden. Let cool, then coarsely chop.

2. In a small bowl, whisk the pomegranate molasses with the vinegar, mustard and honey. Gradually whisk in the olive oil until combined. Season the dressing with salt and pepper.

3. In a large bowl, toss the apples with the spinach, endives, blue cheese, walnuts and some of the dressing. Serve the salad, passing the remaining dressing at the table.

EDITOR'S NOTE

The dressing for this salad gets a fruity, tangy kick from pomegranate molasses, a syrup made of reduced pomegranate juice. Look for it in Middle Eastern and specialty food stores.

GREEN CHILE POSOLE
WITH PORK, P. 34

ISABEL'S CANTINA

ISABEL CRUZ

PUBLISHED BY CLARKSON POTTER, $27

Isabel Cruz grew up in Los Angeles, where her neighbors were from Puerto Rico, Cuba and Mexico as well as Japan and Thailand—the inspiration for her Latin recipes inflected with Asian flavors. Cruz's recipes are lighter than many Latin dishes because her flagship restaurant, Isabel's Cantina, caters to surfers and other body-conscious customers from the San Diego beach just a block away. Recipes like her mahimahi with a zesty sauce combining sake, soy, lemon and roasted jalapeños, or her turkey burger topped with a tangy, smoky chipotle-lime barbecue sauce, rely on vibrant ingredients (such as citrus, chiles and garlic) that deliver lots of flavor without adding fat.

featured recipes Green Chile Posole with Pork; Chipotle-Marinated Grilled Rib Eye; Mahimahi with Jalapeño-Ponzu Sauce

best of the best exclusive Chipotle-Glazed Roast Chicken with Cumin & Red Chile Rub

GREEN CHILE POSOLE WITH PORK

SERVES 6

3 tablespoons olive oil
2½ pounds boneless pork shoulder,
      fat trimmed, cut into 2-inch chunks
Kosher salt
Freshly ground black pepper
1 medium yellow onion, diced
2 garlic cloves, minced
4 cups chicken broth
Roasted Chile Verde Sauce
      (recipe follows)
One 24-ounce can hominy, drained

Posole is a traditional and hearty Mexican stew made with hominy, dried hulled corn kernels. Serve this hearty stew on its own or with pinto beans, grated Monterey Jack cheese, and some fluffy flour tortillas to scoop everything up in.

Heat the olive oil in a large pot over medium-high heat until hot but not smoking. Dry the cubes of pork with a paper towel and season them with salt and pepper. Working in 3 batches, sear the meat on all sides. Don't move the meat around until it has browned well on each side—about 3 minutes per side. Use tongs to transfer the meat to a platter while you sear the next batch.

When all of the meat has been browned, add the onion and garlic to the pot and stir with a wooden spoon until the onion has softened, about 2 minutes. Add the chicken broth, a little at a time, stirring the browned bits off the bottom of the pan. Return the pork to the pot and bring to a gentle simmer. Lower the heat to maintain the simmer and cook for 1 hour, skimming occasionally.

Add the Chile Verde Sauce and the hominy and continue simmering until the pork is exceptionally tender and the soup is thick and richly flavored, about 1 hour more.

The stew can be served immediately or stored, covered, in the refrigerator for up to 3 days. Reheat over medium heat.

Roasted Chile Verde Sauce

MAKES ABOUT 5 CUPS

3   tablespoons olive oil
1   medium yellow onion, diced
5   garlic cloves, minced
4   Anaheim chiles, roasted and chopped (see To Fire-Roast Chiles)
2   poblano chiles, roasted and chopped (see To Fire-Roast Chiles)
1   pound tomatillos, roasted and pureed
3   plum tomatoes, diced
Kosher salt

EDITOR'S NOTE
To prepare the tomatillos for this chile verde sauce, place them on a rimmed baking sheet and roast at 375°F until they begin to crack, 20 to 30 minutes. Transfer to a food processor and puree until smooth.

There are countless ways to use this versatile sauce. Besides using it in Green Chile Posole with Pork, I'll also serve it with tortilla chips.

Heat the oil in a deep, straight-sided sauté pan over medium heat. Add the onion and garlic, and cook until the onion is soft and translucent, about 3 minutes. Add the chiles, the tomatillo puree, and the tomatoes. Bring to a simmer and cook for about 5 minutes to allow the flavors to blend.

Add 1 cup cold water and gently simmer over low heat for about 30 minutes, or until thickened. Season with salt to taste. Serve hot.

The sauce can be stored, covered, in the refrigerator for up to 3 days. Reheat over medium heat before serving.

ISABEL'S TIP This sauce is easy to make but has a few steps. Begin by fire-roasting your chiles and making a tomatillo puree. This can be done in advance, and the roasted chiles and tomatillos can be refrigerated for up to 3 days.

TO FIRE-ROAST CHILES Place the chiles over an open flame (such as on a gas stove top) and roast, turning as needed, until the skins turn a blistery black. Place them in a bowl and cover with plastic wrap for 10 to 15 minutes. The heat will help steam the skins off. Use a paper towel to rub the charred skins from the flesh. Slice each chile in half, remove and discard the seeds, and roughly chop. Remember not to touch your face or your eyes while working with chiles and to wash your hands thoroughly after touching them.

CHIPOTLE-MARINATED GRILLED RIB EYE

SERVES 4

½ cup lime juice (about 4 limes)
3 chipotle chiles in adobo sauce
3 tablespoons packed light
   brown sugar
Kosher salt
1 cup olive oil
2 rib eye steaks (about 16 ounces
   each and 1 inch thick)
Freshly ground black pepper

EDITOR'S NOTE

The spicy and tangy marinade
in this recipe is equally tasty
when used on pork, chicken,
fish or shrimp.

Rib eye is one of my favorite cuts of beef—richly flavorful and tender, this steak on the bone is a cut above. When I serve steak, I want it to be top-notch, and this marinade, with its smoky chipotle kick, never disappoints.

Combine the lime juice, chiles, sugar, and 1½ teaspoons salt in a blender. With the blender running, add the olive oil in a steady stream and continue to blend for about 4 minutes to form a frothy emulsion.

Place the steaks in a large glass baking dish and pour half of the chipotle marinade over them. Turn the steaks to coat. Cover with plastic wrap and refrigerate for at least 2 hours or overnight. Refrigerate the remaining marinade separately.

Remove the reserved marinade and the steaks from the refrigerator 15 to 30 minutes before grilling. Preheat your grill to high.

Remove the steaks from the marinade and season them on both sides with salt and pepper. Place the steaks on the grill and cook, undisturbed, for about 5 minutes, before turning them with tongs. Cook for an additional 5 minutes for medium-rare.

Transfer the steaks to a cutting board and let them rest for 5 minutes before cutting each into 2 servings. Serve the reserved chipotle lime sauce marinade to be spooned over the steaks at the table.

MAHIMAHI WITH JALAPEÑO-PONZU SAUCE

SERVES 4

2 tablespoons olive oil
Four 6-ounce skinless mahimahi fillets
1 teaspoon kosher salt
1 teaspoon freshly cracked
    black pepper
Jalapeño-Ponzu Sauce
1 avocado, thinly sliced

The jalapeño chiles in the sauce are roasted, which gives a little smokiness to their heat and really shakes up a simple, meaty white fish such as mahimahi.

Preheat the oven to 350°F.

In a large ovenproof sauté pan, heat the olive oil over high heat. Season the mahimahi with the salt and pepper. Place the fillets in the pan. Brown for about 2 minutes before flipping and browning the other side for 2 minutes. Transfer the pan to the oven and bake until the fish is opaque throughout, 6 to 8 minutes.

To serve, generously spoon the Jalapeño-Ponzu Sauce over each piece of fish and top with slices of avocado.

Jalapeño-Ponzu Sauce

MAKES ABOUT 1 CUP

2 jalapeños, roasted over an
    open flame and roughly chopped
    (see To Fire-Roast Chiles on p. 35)
½ cup sake
⅓ cup lemon juice (about 3 lemons)
¼ cup soy sauce
1 tablespoon olive oil
3 tablespoons minced fresh ginger
2 tablespoons sugar

Adding jalapeño to traditional Japanese ponzu is a match made in heaven. Bold and delicious, these flavors seem as though they were meant to be together. This also adds zip to a grilled steak.

Combine the jalapeños, sake, lemon juice, soy sauce, olive oil, ginger, and sugar in a food processor or blender and pulse until smooth. Transfer to a small saucepan and simmer for about 3 minutes, or until the raw sake taste begins to mellow.

The sauce can be stored, covered, in the refrigerator for up to 1 week. Warm over low heat before using.

best of the best exclusive

CHIPOTLE-GLAZED ROAST CHICKEN WITH CUMIN & RED CHILE RUB

SERVES 4

One 3½-pound chicken
Kosher salt
2 small chipotle chiles in adobo sauce
2 tablespoons fresh orange juice
2 tablespoons fresh lime juice
2 tablespoons honey
1 small garlic clove, peeled
7 tablespoons extra-virgin olive oil
1½ teaspoons ground cumin
1½ teaspoons New Mexico chile powder

EDITOR'S NOTE

New Mexico chiles, which turn red when they ripen, are dried and ground into a relatively mild, all-purpose chile powder available at specialty stores and from kalustyans.com. Substitute any pure red chile powder (avoid chile blends).

1. Set the chicken on a work surface and rub 1 tablespoon of kosher salt under the skin, on the skin and in the cavity. Place the chicken in a roasting pan, cover and refrigerate for 2 hours.

2. Meanwhile, in a food processor, puree the chipotles with the orange juice, lime juice, honey and garlic. With the motor on, gradually pour in 6 tablespoons of the olive oil and process until blended. Season the chipotle sauce with salt.

3. Preheat the oven to 375°F. In a small bowl, mix the cumin with the chile powder. Rub the chicken all over with the remaining 1 tablespoon of olive oil, then season with the chile powder mixture, rubbing it under and over the skin. Roast the chicken for 1 hour, until the skin is crisp and the chicken is almost fully cooked.

4. Increase the oven temperature to 425°F. Brush the chicken with ¼ cup of the chipotle sauce and roast for about 12 minutes longer, until the skin is golden brown and a thermometer inserted between the thigh and breast registers 165°F. Transfer the chicken to a cutting board and let rest for 5 minutes. Carve the chicken and pass the remaining chipotle sauce at the table.

COD WITH EARLY FALL VEGETABLES, P. 42

THE YOUNG MAN & THE SEA

DAVID PASTERNACK & ED LEVINE

PUBLISHED BY ARTISAN, $35

Dave Pasternack, the chef at the seafood-centric Italian restaurant Esca in New York City, doesn't just cook fish: He catches it, cleans it, fillets it and debones it. An obsessed fisherman, Pasternack has a deep knowledge of seafood that comes through clearly in his recipes, which range from *crudo* (Italy's answer to sushi) to pastas to grilled dishes. His style is direct, approachable and authoritative. In a section on mahimahi, for instance, he shares this observation: "I've caught a lot of mahimahi in my day. They don't play hard to get. In fact, I would have to say mahimahi are pretty stupid. You catch one and reel it halfway onto the boat, and the others follow it."

featured recipes Cod with Early Fall Vegetables; Grilled Snapper with Almond-Oregano Pesto; Flounder with Baby Eggplant, Oven-Dried Tomatoes & Grilled Sweet Onions; Grilled Tuna & Panzanella

best of the best exclusive Rigatoni with White Anchovies & Ricotta

COD WITH EARLY FALL VEGETABLES

SERVES 4

- 2 small turnips, peeled
- 1 medium carrot, peeled
- 1 medium parsnip, peeled
- 1 small zucchini
- ¼ cup extra-virgin olive oil
- Sea salt
- Freshly ground black pepper
- Four 6-ounce cod fillets, about 1¾ inches thick, skin on
- 1 cup Wondra
- 3 tablespoons canola oil

EDITOR'S NOTE

Wondra is a fine white flour favored by Southern cooks for thickening gravies. Here, it coats the fish lightly, without clumping, creating a crisp, golden crust when fried. Wondra is available at most supermarkets.

In the fall, cod is at its firm-fleshed best, and when you combine the fish with some early fall vegetables the results are quite spectacular. This is an easy, versatile dish that's nevertheless worthy of being served to your family or company.

Preheat the oven to 350°F.

Cut all the vegetables into ¾-inch chunks. Place them on a baking sheet, pour the olive oil over, and season with 1 teaspoon each salt and pepper. Toss the vegetables to combine, then spread them into a single layer. Roast in the oven until the vegetables are very tender when pierced with the tip of a knife, about 45 minutes. Transfer to a serving platter and keep warm.

Raise the oven temperature to 400°F.

Dry the cod fillets with paper towels. Season the flour with salt and pepper, then lightly dredge the skin side of the cod fillets in it. Heat the canola oil in a large, preferably nonstick, ovenproof sauté pan until the oil is almost smoking. Add the fillets, skin side down, and sear for 4 minutes, until evenly browned. Turn and cook for 3 to 4 minutes more, then transfer to the hot oven. Continue cooking until the fish begins to flake when you press your finger into it, 4 to 5 minutes.

Serve the cod over the roasted vegetables family-style. Be sure to put a bottle of high-quality extra-virgin olive oil and a dish of sea salt on the table so diners can season their plates.

GRILLED SNAPPER WITH ALMOND-OREGANO PESTO

SERVES 2

One 2-pound snapper, scales
    and fins removed, gutted
  4   parsley stems
  2   slices lemon
  1   clove garlic, crushed
  ¼   cup extra-virgin olive oil
Sea salt
Freshly ground black pepper
Almond-Oregano Pesto (recipe follows)

The Sicilians grow almonds and oregano, and they use them together in many dishes. So I started playing around with the two ingredients after a recent trip to Sicily, and this recipe is the result. Unlike Genovese pesto, this one contains no cheese. If you want to sweeten the dish just a tad, use orange juice instead of lemons. You can also substitute pine nuts or hazelnuts for the almonds, and the dish will turn out just as well. But walnuts might be a little too pungent and earthy.

Prepare a charcoal fire and heat the grill over it.

Dry the fish with paper towels. Stuff the cavity with the parsley stems, lemon slices, and garlic. Rub the fish on both sides with olive oil (use about 2 tablespoons per side) and season with salt and pepper.

When the coals are white-hot, place the fish over the medium-high part of the fire (where you can hold your hand above the coals for, say, 4 seconds). If the flames jump to touch the fish, move it to a cooler part of the grill. Grill the fish for 8 to 10 minutes per side. The skin should be charred but not blackened. The flesh of the fish, when touched, should gently break away under the skin.

Fillet the fish and transfer to two serving plates. Spoon a few tablespoons of the pesto over each piece just before serving.

continued on p. 44

MAKES 1¼ CUPS

- ¾ cup blanched whole almonds
- 2 cloves garlic
- 1 fresh anchovy fillet
- 1 tablespoon coarse sea salt, plus additional for finishing
- 1 cup oregano leaves
- ¼ cup lemon juice
- ¼ cup freshly squeezed blood orange juice
- ¾ cup extra-virgin olive oil
- Freshly ground black pepper

Almond-Oregano Pesto

Toast the almonds. Using a mortar and pestle or a small food processor, pound or process the nuts to small pieces (but not a powder). Transfer to a small mixing bowl and set aside.

Combine the garlic, anchovy fillet, and 1 teaspoon of the salt and pound into a paste. Add the oregano leaves ¼ cup at a time along with one-quarter of the remaining salt each time. Continue to pound the ingredients to a fine paste. Add the paste to the almonds, stirring to combine. Add the lemon juice, blood orange juice, and olive oil, and combine well. Season with salt and freshly ground black pepper.

Use immediately or store in an airtight container in the refrigerator. If making ahead, drizzle some additional olive oil over the pesto to help it keep its color.

Dave Pasternack fishes the waters around New York City.

FLOUNDER WITH BABY EGGPLANT, OVEN-DRIED TOMATOES & GRILLED SWEET ONIONS

SERVES 4

8 baby Italian eggplant, halved lengthwise
Sea salt
Extra-virgin olive oil
4 sprigs rosemary
2 Maui onions, cut into ½-inch slices
Freshly ground black pepper
1 cup Wondra
3 large eggs
Four 5-ounce flounder fillets
¼ cup canola oil
3 tablespoons unsalted butter
Oven-Dried Tomatoes (recipe follows)

The key to this summery dish is to find small eggplant with tender skins and without seeds. The tomatoes add a little acidity that balances the richness of the rest of the dish, and the grilled sweet onions add great texture and sweetness. Leave the onions crunchy, and don't cook them too long. I add a little butter to the pan after I've put the fish in just to give the flounder a luxurious taste.

Sprinkle the cut side of the eggplant with salt. Layer them face down in a colander for 30 minutes to drain some of their water.

Preheat the oven to 350°F.

Place the eggplant, cut side up, on a baking sheet and drizzle liberally with olive oil. Break the sprigs of rosemary into pieces and place them on top of the eggplant. Transfer to the oven and bake until very tender, 30 to 35 minutes.

While the eggplant are cooking, lightly coat the onion slices with olive oil and sprinkle with salt and pepper. Grill over a charcoal fire or heat in a grill pan over a medium-high flame for 3 minutes per side.

Set two wide shallow bowls near the stove. In one, season the flour with 1 teaspoon each salt and pepper. In the other, lightly beat the eggs. Dredge each flounder in the seasoned flour, then dip in the beaten egg. Set each aside on a baking sheet.

In a large, preferably nonstick, sauté pan, heat the canola oil over a medium-high flame until hot but not smoking. Add the butter. When the foam subsides, add the fillets. As they sizzle, carefully use your fingertips to press them down, giving them full contact with the pan. After 2 minutes, give them a quarter turn to the right. Cook until golden brown, 3 to 4 minutes per side. Transfer the cooked fillets to a paper-towel-lined plate and season immediately with salt and pepper. Serve with the Oven-Dried Tomatoes, eggplant, and a few slices of grilled onion.

continued on p. 48

THE YOUNG MAN & THE SEA

DAVID PASTERNACK
& ED LEVINE

SERVES 4

1 pound plum or Roma tomatoes
¼ cup extra-virgin olive oil
Leaves of 2 sprigs thyme
Sea salt
Freshly ground black pepper

EDITOR'S NOTE
You might want to double
the recipe for the Oven-Dried
Tomatoes, which keep for several
days in the fridge and are very
versatile. They make a fast,
tasty pasta sauce when chopped
and stirred with sautéed garlic.

Oven-Dried Tomatoes

Where I live and cook, in the Northeast, the vine-ripened tomato season is really short. So the way I compensate is by making these Oven-Dried Tomatoes, which sweeten just about any plum or Roma tomato you can find year-round.

Preheat the oven to 300°F.

Bring a large pot of water to a boil and prepare a bowl of ice water near the stove. Use a paring knife to score an X on the bottom of each tomato, and use the tip of the knife to carve out the stem end.

Put the tomatoes in the boiling water for 3 minutes, then use a slotted spoon to transfer them to the ice bath. Starting at the X, peel the skins away from the flesh.

Cut each tomato in half lengthwise, and remove and discard the seeds. Place the flesh in a mixing bowl. Add the olive oil and thyme, and season with salt and pepper. Toss to thoroughly coat the tomatoes. Place them, cut side down, on a foil-lined baking sheet. Pour any excess dressing over them and then bake for 1½ hours. When finished, the tomatoes should have shrunk and become a brighter shade of red.

The tomatoes can be used immediately or stored in the refrigerator in an airtight container for 3 days. Let come to room temperature before using.

GRILLED TUNA & PANZANELLA

SERVES 4

1 loaf rustic peasant bread,
crusts removed
Extra-virgin olive oil
Sea salt
Freshly ground black pepper
⅓ cup Chianti vinegar
1 red bell pepper
1 yellow bell pepper
2 large heirloom or vine-ripened
beefsteak tomatoes, cut into chunks
1 pint cherry tomatoes, halved
6 plum tomatoes, cut into spears
1 large or 2 medium cucumbers,
peeled, seeded, and diced
1 small red onion, diced (about ¼ cup)
¼ cup capers (preferably salt-packed)
¼ cup pitted Gaeta olives
¼ cup basil leaves (preferably
opal basil)
¼ cup flat-leaf parsley leaves
Four 6-ounce tuna steaks, about
1¾ inches thick

Panzanella is the classic Tuscan salad of day-old bread and tomatoes that, when made properly, ends up wet and vinegary yet still crunchy. The best one I've ever had was in Porto Ercules, a cute little fishing village. For this dish I use local heirloom tomatoes that I either grow myself in my little garden or buy from my main tomato guy, Tim Starks. You don't have to use heirloom tomatoes, but for this dish I would definitely use vine-ripened tomatoes. Cardboardy, tasteless out-of-season tomatoes that have been picked green, gassed to turn red, and then trucked hundreds or thousands of miles will have a seriously deleterious effect on this dish. But feel free to substitute swordfish for the tuna.

Preheat the oven to 250°F.

Cut the bread into large (1½ to 2 inch) cubes; you should have at least twenty-four croutons. Place the cubes on a baking sheet and drizzle with olive oil. Season with salt and pepper and place in the oven until the bread is dry and crunchy, about 30 minutes. (These can be made a day ahead and kept in a paper bag.)

Combine the Chianti vinegar with ⅔ cup olive oil. Season with ½ teaspoon salt and ½ teaspoon black pepper. Set aside.

continued on p. 50

Roast the peppers over an open flame; this can be done directly on the stove top over a burner or over a charcoal fire. Turn the peppers so that the skin blackens and blisters all the way around. Put the roasted peppers in a bowl and cover with plastic wrap (the heat will help steam off the skin). When they are cool enough to handle, use your fingers to peel away the charred skin. Cut the peppers in half, remove the seeds, and then dice. Set aside.

Place all the cut-up tomatoes in a colander over a bowl for about an hour to drain off some of their liquid. Meanwhile, in a large mixing bowl, combine the diced peppers, cucumber, red onion, capers, olives, basil, and parsley.

Start a charcoal fire, heating the grill over it so that it's very hot.

Rub the tuna steaks on both sides with olive oil and season with salt and pepper. When the coals are white-hot, place the fish over the medium-high part of the fire (where you can hold your hand above the coals for, say, 4 seconds). If the flames jump to touch the fish, move them to a cooler part of the grill. Grill the fish for 5 to 6 minutes per side. When finished, the fish should feel like the fleshy part of your palm. Transfer the cooked fish to a serving platter.

Add the tomatoes and the croutons to the salad ingredients. Whisk the reserved oil and vinegar, and dress the salad, tossing gently but thoroughly. Serve the salad on a platter rather than in a bowl (the weight of the tomatoes can be crushing). Self-service, family-style.

best of the best exclusive

RIGATONI WITH WHITE ANCHOVIES & RICOTTA

SERVES 6

3 tablespoons extra-virgin olive oil
1 small onion, finely chopped
2 garlic cloves, minced
12 marinated white anchovy fillets
(1½ ounces), coarsely chopped
Pinch of crushed red pepper
2¼ cups canned tomato sauce
¼ cup fresh ricotta cheese
1 tablespoon unsalted butter
Kosher salt and freshly ground pepper
1 pound rigatoni

EDITOR'S NOTE

This full-flavored pasta is perfect for anchovy lovers—the rich, tangy flavor of the fish dominates. White anchovies marinated in oil and vinegar, a Spanish tapa called *boquerones*, have a brighter taste and more tender texture than salt-cured anchovies preserved in oil. *Boquerones* are available at some specialty stores, good deli counters and tienda.com.

1. Bring a large pot of salted water to a boil. Meanwhile, in a large, deep skillet, heat 2 tablespoons of the olive oil. Add the onion and garlic and cook over moderate heat until the onion is translucent, about 8 minutes. Stir in the anchovies and crushed red pepper and cook until the anchovies begin to break apart, about 1 minute. Add the tomato sauce and simmer over moderately high heat until thickened, about 5 minutes. Stir in the ricotta and butter and season the sauce with salt and pepper.

2. Cook the rigatoni until al dente; drain. Add the rigatoni to the sauce and cook over low heat, tossing until coated, about 1 minute. Drizzle the rigatoni with the remaining 1 tablespoon of olive oil, transfer to bowls and serve.

Alice Waters aims to help novice cooks in her latest book.

THE ART OF SIMPLE FOOD

ALICE WATERS

PUBLISHED BY CLARKSON POTTER, $35

Alice Waters, the legendary chef and local- and seasonal-cooking advocate behind Berkeley's Chez Panisse, has written nine cookbooks, but this is the first that doesn't aim to reproduce her restaurant recipes; instead, she looks to help the novice cook master straightforward dishes. This is her take on the basics, with lessons on everything from poaching an egg to making tart dough. Her recipes are written in an old-fashioned style—instead of a recipe list at the beginning, each ingredient is called out in the step-by-step instructions—which makes the cooking pace seem slower and more relaxed. Her Baked Wild Salmon with Herb Butter is fresh-tasting and delectable, and her Cheese & Pasta Gratin (a.k.a. mac and cheese) is exactly as it should be: cheesy and gooey on the inside and crispy on top.

featured recipes Baked Wild Salmon with Herb Butter; Sweet Corn Soup; Cheese & Pasta Gratin

BAKED WILD SALMON WITH HERB BUTTER

SERVES 4

EDITOR'S NOTE
Buy wild Alaskan salmon
to be sure you're getting
sustainable seafood.
In general, wild salmon
is leaner, and has more
flavor as well.

Salmon fillets have easy-to-spot pin bones—a row of thin white rib-like bones that extends from behind the gills to the fish's midsection. Rub your fingers over the flesh to locate these bones; use a pair of needle-nosed pliers to pull them out of the flesh.

Prepare:
   ½ cup Herb Butter (recipe follows)

Pull any pin bones from:
   1 to 1½ pounds wild salmon fillet, cut into 4- to 6-ounce pieces
Refrigerate until ready to cook.

Preheat the oven to 425°F and remove the Herb Butter from the refrigerator to soften.

Season the salmon with:
   Salt
   Fresh-ground black pepper

Oil a baking dish or a rimmed baking sheet and place the pieces of salmon in it, skin side down. Brush or drizzle with oil. Bake until the flesh is just set and still pink in the center, 7 to 10 minutes, depending on the thickness of the fillets. Spoon some of the soft Herb Butter over each piece of fish and pass the rest in a small bowl.

VARIATIONS

Add 4 chopped salt-packed anchovy fillets to the Herb Butter.

Another way to bake salmon is to slow roast it. Keep the salmon in one piece with its skin on. Oil a baking dish or a rimmed baking sheet and cover the bottom with a layer of fresh herb sprigs. Place the seasoned salmon skin side down on the herbs. Oil the top of the salmon and bake at 225°F for about 30 minutes. The salmon will be just set and incredibly succulent and tender. This is delicious served at room temperature with a vinaigrette made with lemon juice and zest.

If you have access to fresh fig leaves, this is a must. Although the leaf is not eaten, it suffuses the fish with a delightful coconut aroma. Season and oil the salmon fillets, wrap each piece in a clean fig leaf, and bake as above.

Herb Butter

MAKES ABOUT ¾ CUP

Stir together in a small bowl, mixing well:

    8 tablespoons (1 stick) butter, softened
    ½ cup chopped herbs (such as parsley, chervil, and chives)
    1 garlic clove, finely chopped
    Squeeze of lemon juice
    Salt and fresh-ground black pepper
    A pinch of cayenne

Taste and adjust the salt and lemon as needed.

SWEET CORN SOUP

MAKES 1½ QUARTS; SERVES 4

*This is a no-fail soup as long as you have fresh sweet corn.
I make it all summer and vary it with different garnishes
through the season.*

Melt in a heavy-bottomed pot over medium heat:
   4 tablespoons (½ stick) butter

Add:
   1 onion, diced

Cook until soft, without browning, about 15 minutes.
Season with:
   Salt

Meanwhile, shuck:
   5 ears corn

Cut the kernels from the cobs. Add the kernels to the
cooked onions and cook for 2 to 3 minutes. Cover with:
   1 quart water

Bring to a boil. Immediately lower the heat to a simmer
and cook until the corn is just done, about 5 minutes.
Remove from the heat and puree in small batches in
a blender. (Be careful when blending hot soup in a jug
blender and always make sure there is an air vent to
allow the steam to escape.) Strain the soup through
a medium-mesh strainer to remove any tough skins.
Taste and adjust for salt as needed.

VARIATIONS

Garnish with crème fraîche seasoned with chopped savory, salt, and pepper.

Garnish with chopped nasturtium petals or nasturtium butter (chopped nasturtium petals worked into soft butter seasoned with salt and pepper).

Garnish with a puree of roasted sweet or chile pepper enriched with butter or cream.

CHEESE & PASTA GRATIN

SERVES 4

This gratin (macaroni and cheese by another name) is good to make when you find yourself with the ends of several types of cheeses. Almost any cheese works, except mozzarella, which gets a little stringy, and blue cheeses, which can take over the dish. I love Gruyère for macaroni and cheese, and cheddar, Jack, and Cantal are all good, too.

Melt, in a heavy skillet:

3 tablespoons butter

Add:

3 tablespoons flour

Cook over very low heat, stirring with a whisk for 3 minutes. The roux should bubble gently.

Whisking constantly, add, little by little:

2½ cups milk

Continue whisking until the sauce has the consistency of thick cream. Add:

Salt to taste

Raise the heat to medium, switch to a wooden spoon, and stir continuously until the sauce begins to simmer. Lower the heat and cook, stirring occasionally, for 10 minutes.

Melt in a heavy ovenproof skillet:
   1 tablespoon butter

Add:
   1½ cups fresh bread crumbs

Toss the crumbs to coat with butter and toast in a 350°F oven for 10 to 15 minutes, stirring them every 5 minutes, until lightly browned.

Turn off the heat under the white sauce and stir in:
   8 ounces grated cheese

Cook al dente in abundant salted boiling water:
   ¾ pound short-cut pasta (macaroni, fusilli, penne)

Drain and pour into a buttered gratin dish. Pour the cheese sauce over the pasta and mix until it is well coated. Taste for salt, and adjust as needed. Scatter the toasted bread crumbs over the top and bake in a 400°F oven for 15 minutes, or until the crumbs are golden brown and the sauce is bubbling.

VARIATIONS

Stir together the pasta and the sauce and serve right away instead of finishing in the oven.

Stir in diced ham or prosciutto.

INCREDIBLE BAKED LAMB SHANKS, P. 62

COOK WITH JAMIE

JAMIE OLIVER

PUBLISHED BY HYPERION, $37.50

British TV chef Jamie Oliver's latest book—inspired, no doubt, by his success teaching disadvantaged young people how to cook at his three "Fifteen" restaurants—is a primer of sorts aimed at explaining the culinary basics to people at every skill level. Many of his delightful recipes are Italian inspired, but there are global influences, too, as the book is driven not by a type of cuisine but by an interest in finding the best ingredients. In his candid, colorful voice, Oliver notes, "I want you to shop well and recognize when you're being ripped off by a market seller or a supermarket, when you're being sold rubbish or average stuff. But more than that, I want you to have fun. And I want you to understand a bit more about cooking methods—slow, fast, how and why." His risotto flavored with tomato, basil and ricotta and his sweet, thyme-scented onion gratin are fabulous—and slightly more ambitious than might be expected from a 101-type book.

featured recipes Incredible Baked Lamb Shanks; Scotch Stovies; The Best Onion Gratin; Tomato, Basil & Ricotta Risotto

Find more recipes by Jamie Oliver at foodandwine.com/oliver.

INCREDIBLE BAKED LAMB SHANKS

SERVES 4

  6 sprigs of fresh rosemary
5½ ounces cold butter
 15 fresh sage leaves
  2 sprigs of fresh thyme,
     leaves picked
Sea salt and freshly ground black pepper
  4 lamb shanks, preferably free-range or
     organic, crown- or French-trimmed
 12 cloves of garlic, unpeeled
  2 large carrots, peeled and
     finely sliced
  1 onion, peeled and
     finely sliced
  1 leek, washed, halved and
     finely sliced
Olive oil
  2 wineglasses of white wine

Many people have a real affection for lamb shanks, thinking of them as a bit of a treat. I've cooked them for years and really love this particular style of baking them because it's so easy and comforting—almost like wrapping up a baking potato to put on the bonfire. By using simple root veg and a flavored butter, and by tightly squeezing the aluminum foil around each shank, the most is made of the flavor of the meat without having to cover it in spices or tomatoes or anything like that. It's very easy to prep the shanks for this dish and I think they look cool enough to be a lovely main course for a dinner party.

The shanks should be eaten with all the veggies and any buttery juices. They're really good served with creamy mashed potato and steamed greens to contrast with the roasting stickiness of the lamb.

Preheat your oven to 400°F. Pick the leaves off 2 sprigs of rosemary, whiz them with the butter, most of the sage and the thyme in a food processor and season with salt and pepper. Using a small knife, take one of the lamb shanks and cut between the meat and the bone from the base of the shank upwards. You want to create a hole big enough to put your finger in, making a sort of pocket. Do this to all the shanks and divide the flavored butter between them, pushing it into the pockets. This will give a wonderful flavor to the heart of the shanks.

Tear off four arm-length pieces of aluminum foil and fold each in half to give you four large-sized pieces of foil. Divide the garlic and veg between them, making a pile in the middle of each square. Rub the lamb shanks with olive oil and season with salt and pepper, then put one on top of each pile of veg and a sprig of rosemary and a few sage leaves on top of that. Carefully pull up the sides of the foil around the shank and pour a swig of wine into each. Gather the foil around the bone, pinching it together tightly. Any excess foil can be torn or cut off with scissors. Repeat for all 4 shanks, then place the foil parcels in a baking pan with the bones facing up. Put in the preheated oven for 2½ hours or until the meat is as tender as can be. Serve the parcels in the middle of the table so that your guests can open them up themselves.

WINE SUGGESTION Spanish red—Rioja

SCOTCH STOVIES

SERVES 4

2 onions, peeled and finely sliced
Lard or butter
Olive oil
A few sprigs of fresh thyme,
    leaves picked
Sea salt and freshly ground black pepper
2¼ pounds floury potatoes,
    peeled and cut into chunks
A bunch of watercress,
    washed and dried
A handful of celery leaves, chopped

EDITOR'S NOTE
If you love watercress,
use two bunches here,
since it wilts down to nearly
nothing when cooked.

Scotch stovies is a classic potato dish from up north and, like in parts of Italy, different areas think that they have the best recipe! This is one of my favorite ways of doing it as I think it brings the best flavor out of the potatoes; and the celery leaves and watercress give a lightness which means it's good with fish dishes. If you've never tried them, you must give these a bash.

Very slowly fry the onions with the butter or lard and the olive oil, thyme and a little salt and pepper for 10 to 15 minutes until lightly golden and soft. Add your potatoes and a pint of water. Simmer with a lid on and stir occasionally until the potatoes have gone mushy. Stir and scrape any sticky bits off the bottom of the pan and mix them in. You can mash the mixture up if you like, or leave it as it is with bigger and smaller lumps. Correct the seasoning, then stir the watercress and celery leaves through the mash and serve.

THE BEST ONION GRATIN

SERVES 4

 4 medium red onions, peeled
    and quartered
Olive oil
Sea salt and freshly ground black pepper
 8 sprigs of fresh thyme,
    leaves picked
 2 cloves of garlic, peeled
    and sliced
A small wineglass of white wine
 4 tablespoons crème fraîche
1¾ ounces Gruyère cheese,
    grated
1¾ ounces Parmesan cheese,
    grated

EDITOR'S NOTE

If you don't have a small
wineglass on hand, figure
about ½ cup (4 ounces) of
wine for this recipe.

I always think it's a pleasure to write a recipe that celebrates onions as vegetables in their own right, and not just treat them as something that you use as the base of a stew or soup. Make this gratin and it's bound to be the talk of the meal because it's got ballsy flavor and sweetness. To rev the recipe up a bit, try using a mixture of white, red and button onions or shallots. But I'll leave that up to you.

Preheat the oven to 400°F. Break the onion quarters apart to give you little "petals." Place these in an ovenproof glass or earthenware oven dish. Drizzle with a couple of glugs of olive oil and a pinch of salt and pepper, and toss in your thyme and garlic. Mix up well, add your white wine, cover with a double layer of aluminum foil, wrap tightly and place in the preheated oven. Bake for 45 minutes, then remove the dish from the oven, take the foil off and pop the dish back in the oven for 15 minutes to start caramelizing. Once the onion is looking lightly golden, stir in your crème fraîche and sprinkle over your Gruyère and Parmesan. Turn the oven down to 350°F and let the gratin tick away for about 15 minutes or until golden and gorgeous. You can eat this straight away, or cool it down and flash it under the broiler later.

TOMATO, BASIL & RICOTTA RISOTTO

SERVES 8

FOR THE TOMATOES

4 large handfuls of interesting ripe
tomatoes, seeds removed and flesh
roughly chopped
A splash of good red wine vinegar
A good lug of oil
Sea salt and freshly ground black pepper

1x basic risotto recipe (recipe follows)
9 ounces crumbly ricotta cheese
Extra-virgin olive oil
1 dried red chile, crumbled
1 teaspoon dried oregano
Sea salt and freshly ground black pepper
1¼ pints hot vegetable or
chicken stock
7 tablespoons butter
1 to 2 handfuls of freshly grated Parmesan
cheese, plus a block for grating
1 large bunch of fresh basil,
leaves picked
Extra-virgin olive oil

EDITOR'S NOTE

For a delicious, summery
bruschetta, serve the baked
ricotta and marinated
tomatoes from this recipe on
slices of grilled Italian bread.

Two things are especially important when it comes to making this risotto: first, try and get hold of different shapes and colors of tomatoes—there are lots of varieties available these days—and second, make sure you get the right type of ricotta. It should be snow-white and really crumbly. Unfortunately, the ricotta that you tend to get in the supermarkets is a bit like semolina and just horrible, so unless you can get some lovely crumbly white ricotta, then use a mild crumbly goat's cheese instead.

Preheat the oven to 350°F. Marinate your tomatoes in the red wine vinegar, olive oil, and a pinch of salt and pepper. Make your basic risotto recipe, then place the ricotta in a small baking pan, rub it with extra-virgin olive oil, sprinkle over the chile and oregano, season it and place in the preheated oven for 10 minutes until golden brown.

Meanwhile, place a large saucepan on a medium to high heat and pour in half the stock, followed by your risotto base and two-thirds of the tomatoes. Stirring all the time, gently bring to the boil, then turn down the heat and simmer until almost all the stock has been absorbed. Add the rest of the stock a ladleful at a time until the rice is cooked. You might not need all your stock. Be careful not to overcook the rice—check it throughout cooking to make sure it ends up soft, creamy and oozy. And the overall texture should be slightly looser than you think you want it.

continued on p. 68

Turn off the heat, beat in your butter and Parmesan and tear in the larger basil leaves, reserving the small ones for sprinkling over before serving. Check the seasoning and add salt and pepper if needed, then stir in your baked ricotta and marinated tomatoes. Put a lid on the pan and leave the risotto to rest for a minute before taking it to the table. Either let everyone help themselves, or divide the risotto between individual serving plates. Sprinkle over the little basil leaves, drizzle with a little extra-virgin olive oil and put a block of Parmesan on the table for grating over.

WINE SUGGESTION French white—Chenin Blanc

A Basic Recipe for Making Risotto

Here's the basic risotto recipe. Now, this recipe will take you up to a point where the rice is 75 percent ready, and all that's left to do is finish it off. The idea is that if you make this base in advance, you can then spread the rice out on a pan until you're ready to use it (or you can launch straight into flavoring it, in which case the pan won't be needed). Remember to have a large clean pan, rubbed with a little olive oil, right by the stove. It's important that it's large, so the rice can be spread thinly, meaning it will cool down faster and not end up cooking itself. If you don't have a big pan in the house, use a couple of small ones instead.

SERVES 8

1¾ pints vegetable or chicken stock
2 tablespoons olive oil
1 tablespoon butter
1 large onion, peeled and finely chopped
4 to 5 sticks of celery, trimmed and finely chopped
1 pound 6 ounces risotto rice
9 fluid ounces vermouth or dry white wine

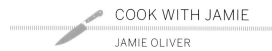

STAGE 1 Have a large oiled pan on hand. Bring the stock to a simmer in a saucepan. Put the olive oil and butter in a separate large pan, add the onion and celery and cook very gently for about 15 minutes, without coloring, until soft. Add the rice (it will sizzle!) and turn up the heat. Don't let the rice or veg catch on the bottom of the pan, so keep it moving.

STAGE 2 Quickly pour in the vermouth or wine. You will smell the alcohol immediately, so keep stirring all the time until it has evaporated, leaving the rice with a lovely perfume.

STAGE 3 Add the stock to the rice a ladle at a time, stirring and waiting until it has been fully absorbed before adding the next. Turn the heat down to low so the rice doesn't cook too quickly, otherwise the outside of each grain will be stodgy and the inside hard and nutty (you don't want to cook it too slowly either, or it will turn into rice pudding!), and continue to add ladlefuls of stock until it has all been absorbed. This should take about 14 to 15 minutes and give you rice that is beginning to soften but is still a little al dente.

STAGE 4 Tip the part-cooked rice out on to the waiting oiled pan. Spread it out evenly, about 1 inch thick, on the pan and then put it somewhere cold to cool down. When the rice has lost all its heat, scrape it up carefully with a rubber spatula and store it in a Tupperware container with a lid in the fridge until you're ready to use it. It will keep for a couple of days.

MEDITERRANEAN

FALL SALAD, P. 74

CRISTINA'S TUSCAN TABLE

CRISTINA CECCATELLI COOK

PUBLISHED BY GIBBS SMITH, $29.95

Cristina Ceccatelli Cook grew up in Tuscany, but after falling in love with an American, she moved to Sun Valley, Idaho, where she opened Cristina's Restaurant 15 years ago. Cook re-creates the restaurant's classic Italian dishes in this, her second cookbook. The sheer simplicity of her recipes makes this book incredibly appealing. There aren't a lot of wordy instructions and lengthy steps; cooking directions and ingredient lists are nicely succinct. Two standout dishes: a salad with an autumn-inspired combination of figs, burrata (cream-filled mozzarella), pecans and lettuce, and a spicy spaghetti with eggplant.

featured recipes Fall Salad; Celery, Hazelnut & Pecorino Salad; Spaghetti with Spicy Eggplant; Ziti & Vodka Sauce

best of the best exclusive Black Cod in Salsa Verde

FALL SALAD

SERVES 6

1 head butter lettuce, outer
  leaves removed
¼ pound fresh arugula
18 fresh figs, halved
1 burrata (about 1 pound; see Note)
  or fresh mozzarella, torn or sliced
½ cup pecan or walnut halves
Lemon Vinaigrette
Freshly cracked black pepper
Few drops vino cotto (optional)

EDITOR'S NOTE
Vino cotto, a tangy-sweet liquid made
by aging reduced grape must (freshly
pressed juice) in wood barrels, is
best used for drizzling, like an aged
balsamic. It is available at specialty
stores and from igourmet.com.

MAKES 1 CUP

½ cup extra-virgin olive oil
½ cup freshly squeezed lemon juice
½ cup finely chopped Italian parsley
1 tablespoon brown sugar
Salt and pepper to taste

Add a slice of good bread and forget traditions . . . the grandmothers . . . art . . . Tuscans . . . it's just a simple lunch or dinner!

In a bowl, gently tear butter lettuce and mix with arugula.

On a serving platter, arrange greens, figs, burrata, and nuts. Drizzle with Lemon Vinaigrette, add freshly cracked black pepper, and—if you want to be extravagant—a few drops of vino cotto.

NOTE Burrata is a cheese formed by wrapping a creamy stracciatella center with a fleshy outer layer of fresh mozzarella, resulting in a large ball weighing one pound. This robust cheese is creamy and dense and is best enjoyed naturally or dressed with a little salt, black pepper, and olive oil. Arugula is a good match for burrata.

Lemon Vinaigrette

Lemon Vinaigrette is good warm or cold, on fish, salads, chicken, or fruit.

Whisk together all ingredients.

CELERY, HAZELNUT & PECORINO SALAD

SERVES 6

3 celery hearts and tender pale green leaves
2 cups toasted hazelnuts, coarsely crushed
2 pounds brinata (see Note), cut in ½-inch cubes
Lemon Vinaigrette (see recipe on previous page)
30 whole leaves Italian parsley, for garnish
Freshly cracked black pepper

EDITOR'S NOTE
To save the step of skinning hazelnuts, you can buy blanched raw hazelnuts, then proceed with toasting and crushing them as directed here.

Cut celery hearts into ½-inch crescents and coarsely chop the pale green leaves.

In a salad bowl, mix celery, toasted hazelnuts, and brinata. Lightly toss with Lemon Vinaigrette, garnish with parsley leaves, and serve with freshly cracked black pepper.

NOTE Brinata is a young Tuscan pecorino, mild and soft. Its natural, edible rind is encrusted with a delicate white mold, like felt. Brinata is very good served with quince, truffle honey, fig mustard, almond or chestnut honey . . . and, of course, with pears or fava beans.

Toasted Hazelnuts

Preheat oven to 500°F.

On a baking sheet, bake nuts 4 to 5 minutes, then rub with a clean towel until skin is almost all gone. On a flat surface, crush nuts into large pieces. We do it by rocking the bottom of a heavy skillet over the nuts.

SPAGHETTI WITH SPICY EGGPLANT

SERVES 6

2   medium eggplants, skins on,
    cut in 1-inch cubes
1   tablespoon kosher salt
1¼ cups extra-virgin olive oil, divided
4   cups diced fresh tomatoes
10 canned piquillo peppers or
    3 roasted bell peppers, skins and
    seeds removed, cut in ½-inch strips
2   tablespoons minced garlic
2   cups Salsa Rossa or canned
    tomato sauce
1   cup fresh basil leaves, cut in strips
Pinch of hot red pepper flakes
2   tablespoons fresh oregano leaves
2   tablespoons chopped
    Italian parsley
1   pound spaghetti
Shaved Parmigiano

As someone once said, "No man is lonely while eating spaghetti—it requires too much attention!"

Place eggplant in colander, sprinkle with salt, and let rest for one hour.

Pat eggplant dry. In a large skillet, heat ¼ cup olive oil on high. Add in one layer of eggplant and cook until crispy on one side. Do not stir. Turn to crisp other side. Eggplant will shrink and crisp. Repeat until all the eggplant is crispy.

In a wide pot, heat ¼ cup olive oil, add diced tomatoes and peppers, and cook on high, stirring, for about 3 minutes. Lower heat, add garlic, and cook for 2 more minutes. Add eggplant and Salsa Rossa, and cook, stirring gently a couple of times. Add basil, red pepper flakes, oregano, and parsley.

In a large pot, bring salted water to boil and cook spaghetti until al dente. Drain, reserving 2 cups cooking water. Add pasta to sauce and cook over high heat 2 to 3 minutes, adding a little pasta water if needed to keep everything juicy. Serve with shaved Parmigiano.

Salsa Rossa

3   tablespoons extra-virgin olive oil
1   pound very ripe tomatoes,
    coarsely chopped
4   cloves garlic, minced
Pinch of hot red pepper flakes
10 fresh basil leaves, chopped
Salt and pepper to taste

Heat the olive oil in a skillet. Add tomatoes, garlic, and red pepper flakes, and sauté until tomatoes are soft. Stir in fresh basil, and add salt and pepper to taste. Puree or leave chunky.

ZITI & VODKA SAUCE

SERVES 6 TO 8

6 slices pancetta, ⅛ inch thick
1 small yellow onion, quartered
6 cups canned or fresh plum
   tomatoes, pureed
Pinch of hot red pepper flakes
½ cup unflavored vodka
1 cup heavy cream
Salt and pepper to taste
1 pound ziti
¾ cup grated Parmigiano

EDITOR'S NOTE
Any unflavored vodka that
you have on hand will work in
this classic Italian sauce.
The alcohol enhances the flavor
of the tomatoes and red
pepper and then dissipates,
so you don't taste it.

Pasta is "It!" The people's food. Economical, healthy, versatile, and simple.

In a food processor, finely mince pancetta and onion together. Transfer to a heavy sauté pan and cook over medium heat until golden brown, about 15 to 20 minutes.

Add pureed tomatoes and red pepper flakes and simmer on low, partially covered, for 30 minutes. Add vodka and cook 10 more minutes. Slowly add heavy cream and bring back to simmer.

In a large pot, bring salted water to a boil and cook ziti until al dente. Drain, reserving one cup cooking water. Drag ziti in sauce, and cook over high heat 2 to 3 minutes, adding a little water if needed for moisture. Adjust for salt and pepper, and serve with Parmigiano.

best of the best exclusive
BLACK COD IN SALSA VERDE

SERVES 6

- 2 cups flat-leaf parsley leaves
- 2 large garlic cloves
- 1 tablespoon capers plus 1 teaspoon caper brine from the jar
- 1 oil-packed anchovy
- 2 teaspoons red wine vinegar
- ½ cup plus 1 tablespoon extra-virgin olive oil

Kosher salt and freshly ground pepper

- 2 pounds black cod, cut into 6 equal pieces
- 3 tablespoons fresh lemon juice
- 1 tablespoon finely grated lemon zest
- ½ cup dry white wine

EDITOR'S NOTE

This bright, tangy salsa verde is good on many kinds of firm fish, such as Pacific cod.

1. On a cutting board, finely chop the parsley with the garlic, capers and anchovy. Transfer to a small bowl and stir in the caper brine and red wine vinegar. Gradually stir in 7 tablespoons of the olive oil and season the salsa verde with salt and pepper.

2. In a large baking dish, toss the cod with the lemon juice, lemon zest and 2 tablespoons of the salsa verde. Season the fish with salt and pepper. Cover with plastic wrap and let stand for 30 minutes.

3. Preheat the oven to 450°F. In a large ovenproof skillet, heat the remaining 2 tablespoons of olive oil. Add the cod to the skillet, reserving the marinade, and cook over moderately high heat for 2 minutes. Turn the fish and cook for 2 minutes longer. Pour the reserved marinade and the white wine into the skillet and bring to a boil. Transfer the skillet to the oven and bake the fish for 8 minutes, until cooked through. Transfer the cod to plates, spoon the remaining salsa verde over the fish and serve.

SERVE WITH Steamed potatoes.

MAKE AHEAD The salsa verde can be refrigerated for up to 2 days.

The recipes in Martha Rose
Shulman's book rely on olive oils
from around the Mediterranean.

MEDITERRANEAN HARVEST

MARTHA ROSE SHULMAN

PUBLISHED BY RODALE, $39.95

A lot of people who want to eat healthily turn to vegetarian recipes or try the Mediterranean diet; this cookbook lets them do both at the same time. A tome with more than 500 recipes, it's the work of Martha Rose Shulman, who has written over 25 super-reliable cookbooks. Shulman weaves food history, personal anecdotes and recipes into one comprehensive volume covering France, Spain, Italy, Turkey, Greece, North Africa, the Balkans and the Middle East. This is a brainy, engaging compilation, full of colorful and extensive travel notes that give each of the excellent recipes a sense of place.

featured recipes Roasted Eggplant Salad with Feta & Green Peppers; Spring Onion, Garlic & Greens Tart; Barley Risotto with Pesto & Ricotta Salata; Chick Pea Stew

best of the best exclusive Tomato-Lentil Soup

ROASTED EGGPLANT SALAD WITH FETA & GREEN PEPPERS

SERVES 4 TO 6

1½ pounds (about 2 medium) eggplants
2 tablespoons fresh lemon juice
Salt and freshly ground pepper
Pinch cayenne (optional)
¼ cup extra-virgin olive oil
1 small or medium red onion, finely chopped and soaked for 5 to 10 minutes in cold water, then drained and rinsed
1 medium green bell pepper, finely chopped
1 medium tomato, peeled, seeded, and chopped
1 or 2 garlic cloves (to taste), minced or put through a press
½ cup crumbled feta (about 3 ounces)

EDITOR'S NOTE
This finely chopped salad is smooth enough to be served as a dip with warm pita or pita chips, or as an accompaniment to grilled meat.

The textures of the chopped pepper and red onion against the creamy chopped eggplant make this luscious dish unique among eggplant salads. This version has less oil and feta than the traditional Greek salad.

1. Rinse the eggplants and pat dry. Prepare a medium-hot fire in a grill or heat the broiler. Broil or grill the eggplants about 6 inches from the heat, turning often, until the eggplants are soft and the skins are uniformly charred. Remove and place in a covered bowl until cool enough to handle.

2. Cut the eggplants in half lengthwise. Scoop the flesh out and discard the skins. Chop the eggplant, discarding as many seeds as you can, and place in a bowl. Add the lemon juice, salt, ground pepper, cayenne, and olive oil, and toss together. Add the onion, bell pepper, tomato, garlic, and feta, toss again, and serve.

ADVANCE PREPARATION The eggplants can be roasted and tossed with the olive oil and lemon juice a day or two ahead.

SPRING ONION, GARLIC & GREENS TART

SERVES 4 TO 6

Salt
2½ to 3 pounds Swiss chard, stemmed
and washed thoroughly
½ recipe Yeasted Olive Oil Pastry
(recipe follows)
2 tablespoons extra-virgin olive oil
1 pound spring onions, bulbs
and light green parts of the tops
only, chopped
½ head green garlic, cloves (if the
garlic has begun to form them)
separated, peeled, and minced;
or 4 garlic cloves, minced
Freshly ground pepper
3 large eggs, beaten
½ cup milk
½ cup grated Gruyère cheese
¼ cup freshly grated Parmesan

If you've never seen the plump, juicy heads of green garlic that hit Mediterranean markets (and California markets too) in the spring, you've got a real treat in store. Combine the garlic with gently cooked spring onions—those small green onions that you might confuse with scallions, except they're bigger than scallions, and bulbous—and irresistibly generous bunches of Swiss chard that you'll also find at spring farmers' markets. Make this as a tart or a gratin (see the variation that follows).

1. Bring a large pot of water to a boil. Add 1 tablespoon salt and the greens. Blanch for 2 minutes, or until just tender, and transfer to a bowl of cold water. Drain and squeeze out water. Chop coarsely and set aside.

2. Heat the oven to 375°F. Oil a 10-inch tart pan. Roll out the pastry and use to line the pan.

3. Heat the olive oil in a large, heavy nonstick frying pan over medium heat and add the spring onions. Cook, stirring often, until tender and fragrant, 5 to 8 minutes. Stir in the garlic and cook for 2 minutes or so, just until fragrant. Add the chopped greens and stir together. Season with salt and pepper. Remove from the heat and set aside.

continued on p. 84

4. Beat the eggs in a medium bowl. Beat in the milk and
½ teaspoon salt, then stir in the greens and onions.
Add plenty of pepper and stir in the cheeses. Scrape the
filling into the pastry shell. Bake for 30 to 40 minutes, until
firm and beginning to brown on top. Serve hot, warm, or
at room temperature.

ADVANCE PREPARATION The greens can be blanched and
chopped up to 3 days ahead and kept in a covered bowl in
the refrigerator. Step 3 can also be completed several hours
before you assemble the gratin or tart, and the vegetables
held at room temperature. The tart can be made several
hours before serving. Reheat in a 325°F oven for 15 minutes
if desired.

VARIATION *Spring Onion, Garlic & Greens Gratin:* Omit the
crust. Oil a 2-quart gratin dish and scrape in the filling. Bake
as directed above.

Yeasted Olive Oil Pastry

*Yeasted crusts are delicate and tasty, and much easier to
manipulate than short crusts, as they don't crack and tear.
Roll this thin so it doesn't become too bready.*

MAKES ENOUGH FOR ONE 10- OR
11-INCH DOUBLE-CRUSTED TORTE,
ONE GALETTE, OR TWO 10-INCH TARTS

- 2 teaspoons active dry yeast
- ½ cup lukewarm water
- ½ teaspoon sugar
- 1 large egg, at room temperature,
     beaten
- ¼ cup extra-virgin olive oil
- 2 cups unbleached all-purpose flour
     (more as needed)
- ¾ teaspoon salt

1. Dissolve the yeast in the water, add the sugar, and allow
to sit until creamy, about 5 minutes. Beat in the egg and
olive oil. Combine the flour and salt, and stir into the yeast
mixture. You can use a bowl and wooden spoon for this,
or a mixer with the paddle. Work the dough until it comes

EDITOR'S NOTE
Because it is made with yeast,
this pastry makes for an unusual
tart shell—it's softer, chewier and
breadier than the typical crust.
The recipe yields twice the amount
of dough needed for the tart;
freeze the rest to make more tarts
or save it for another use.

together in a coherent mass, adding flour as necessary. Turn out onto a lightly floured surface and knead for a few minutes, adding flour as necessary, until the dough is smooth; do not overwork. Shape into a ball. Place in a lightly oiled bowl, cover tightly with plastic wrap, and allow the dough to rise in a draft-free spot until doubled, about 1 hour.

2. Turn the dough out onto a lightly floured surface, gently knead a couple of times, and cut into 2 equal pieces. Shape each piece into a ball. Cover the dough loosely with plastic wrap and let rest for 5 minutes. Then roll out into thin rounds and use to line lightly oiled pans. If not using right away, freeze the dough to prevent it from rising and becoming too bready. The dough can be transferred directly from the freezer to the oven.

ADVANCE PREPARATION You can make the dough a day ahead and refrigerate. Once rolled out, the dough will keep for a month in the freezer, well wrapped.

VARIATION Substitute ½ cup whole wheat flour for ½ cup of the all-purpose flour.

BARLEY RISOTTO WITH PESTO & RICOTTA SALATA

SERVES 4 TO 6

FOR THE PESTO

2   large garlic cloves, peeled
1   cup tightly packed fresh basil
    or arugula leaves
Salt
¼   cup extra-virgin olive oil
¼   cup freshly grated Parmesan
Freshly ground pepper

FOR THE ORZOTTO

7   cups vegetable broth or chicken
    stock (as needed)
Salt
2   tablespoons extra-virgin olive oil
1   small onion or 2 shallots, minced
1½ cups barley
½   cup dry white wine, such as
    pinot grigio or sauvignon blanc
½   cup grated ricotta salata
Freshly ground pepper

Risotto can be made with other starchy grains, like barley or farro. Barley risotto, which is called orzotto in Italy, is chewier than risotto made with rice. I ate a beautiful one with arugula pesto and ricotta when I was passing through the Abruzzo region of Italy one hot summer. The risotto is equally delicious when the pesto that is stirred in at the end is made with basil.

Serve it in wide soup bowls or on plates, spreading the risotto in a thin layer rather than a mound.

1. MAKE THE PESTO Turn on a processor fitted with the steel blade and drop in the garlic. Scrape down the sides of the food processor bowl, add the basil or arugula and salt (⅛ to ¼ teaspoon), and process until finely chopped. Scrape down the sides once more. Drizzle in the olive oil with the machine running. Process to a paste. Stir in the Parmesan and pepper. Taste and adjust salt.

2. MAKE THE ORZOTTO Put your broth into a saucepan and bring it to a simmer on the stove, with a ladle nearby or in the pot. Make sure that it is well seasoned with salt. It will remain at a simmer the entire time you are making the risotto, and you will add it a ladleful or two at a time to the barley.

3. Heat the oil in a wide, heavy nonstick skillet over medium heat. Add the onion and cook gently until tender and translucent, about 5 minutes. Stir in the barley and stir until the grains become separate.

EDITOR'S NOTE
This recipe calls for barley,
a whole grain that gives
the risotto a nice chewiness.
Pearled barley, which
has been hulled and polished,
can also be used. It cooks
faster and yields a softer,
creamier risotto.

4. Add the wine and cook, stirring, until it has just about evaporated and been absorbed by the barley. Stir in enough of the simmering broth to just cover the barley. The broth should bubble slowly. Cook, stirring often, until it is just about absorbed. Add another ladleful or two of the broth and continue to cook in this fashion, not too fast and not too slowly, adding more broth when the barley is almost dry and stirring often, for 30 to 40 minutes, until the barley is just tender to the bite.

5. Add another ⅓ cup broth to the barley. Stir in the pesto and ricotta salata, and remove from the heat. The mixture should be creamy. Add freshly ground pepper, taste one last time, and adjust salt. Stir once and serve right away.

ADVANCE PREPARATION You can begin up to several hours before serving: Proceed with the recipe and cook halfway through, that is, for about 15 minutes. The barley should still be hard in the middle when you remove it from the heat, and there should not be any liquid in the pan. Spread it in an even layer in the pan and keep it away from the heat until you resume cooking. If the pan is not wide enough for you to spread the barley in a thin layer, then transfer it to a sheet pan. Thirty minutes before serving, resume cooking as instructed.

VARIATION *Barley Risotto with Asparagus or Green Beans & Pesto:* Add ½ pound asparagus or green beans to the risotto. Trim and parboil or steam for 5 minutes, and cut into 1-inch pieces. Stir into the risotto along with the pesto.

CHICK PEA STEW

SERVES 4

2   tablespoons extra-virgin olive oil
2   onions, sliced
4   garlic cloves, chopped
1   teaspoon cumin seeds, crushed
1   teaspoon fennel seeds, crushed
1   teaspoon brown sugar or
    2 teaspoons pomegranate molasses
1   tablespoon white wine vinegar,
    sherry vinegar, or lemon juice
4   tomatoes, peeled and chopped; or
    1 can (14 ounces) tomatoes, drained
    and chopped
½   teaspoon Aleppo pepper
4   ounces leaf spinach
½   pound dried chick peas, cooked and
    drained; or 2 cans (15 ounces each)
    chick peas, rinsed and drained
Salt
¼   cup chopped fresh herbs,
    preferably a mix of flat-leaf parsley,
    dill, and mint
Lemon wedges
Drained yogurt

EDITOR'S NOTE
Greek yogurt is strained (the watery whey is drained out), making it thick and creamy—perfect for serving with this stew. It's available in the dairy section of most markets.

This dish—from Edirne, an early capital of the Ottoman Empire—has all the complexity of the sophisticated palace cooking of Istanbul, with sweet, spicy, and savory overtones and a mixture of mint, dill, and parsley that define the dish as Turkish. Although there are a lot of ingredients in the stew, it's very uncomplicated to cook.

Heat the oil in a large nonstick skillet over medium heat and add the onions. Cook, stirring, until tender, about 5 minutes, and add the garlic, cumin, and fennel seeds. Cook until the onion has colored slightly, 5 to 8 minutes. Add the sugar and stir together for a minute, then stir in the vinegar, tomatoes, and Aleppo pepper. Cook, stirring, until the tomatoes have cooked down a bit, about 10 minutes. Stir in the spinach, chick peas, and salt (about 1 teaspoon). Add enough water so that the dish can simmer. Simmer uncovered over medium heat, stirring often, for 20 to 25 minutes. The stew should be saucy but not watery. Add salt to taste and stir in the herbs. Serve with lemon wedges and yogurt.

ADVANCE PREPARATION This dish keeps well for a few days in the refrigerator, and benefits from being made ahead.

best of the best exclusive

TOMATO-LENTIL SOUP

SERVES 6

- 2 tablespoons extra-virgin olive oil, plus more for drizzling
- 1 onion, cut into ¼-inch dice
- 2 carrots, quartered lengthwise and cut crosswise into ½-inch pieces
- 1 celery rib, halved lengthwise and cut crosswise into ½-inch pieces
- 2 garlic cloves, minced
- 5 cups water
- One 28-ounce can whole tomatoes with their juices
- 1 cup French green lentils (7 ounces), rinsed and drained
- 2 bay leaves
- One 3-inch sprig of rosemary
- Kosher salt and freshly ground pepper
- Shredded Gruyère cheese, for serving

1. In a medium soup pot, heat the 2 tablespoons of olive oil. Add the onion and cook over moderate heat until softened, about 5 minutes. Add the carrots, celery and garlic and cook, stirring occasionally, until tender, about 5 minutes. Add the water, tomatoes with their juices, lentils, bay leaves and rosemary. Bring the soup to a simmer, breaking up the tomatoes with the back of a spoon. Cover and simmer over low heat until the lentils are tender, about 30 minutes.

2. Season the soup with salt and pepper and discard the bay leaves and rosemary sprig. Ladle the soup into bowls, drizzle with olive oil, sprinkle with cheese and serve.

MAKE AHEAD The soup can be refrigerated for up to 3 days.

SWEET MYRTLE
& BITTER HONEY

EFISIO FARRIS

PUBLISHED BY RIZZOLI, $39.95

This cookbook offers an in-depth look at a relatively unexplored part of Italy: the island of Sardinia. The author is Sardinia native Efisio Farris, the chef and owner of Arcodoro in Houston and Arcodoro & Pomodoro in Dallas and an importer of Sardinian ingredients to the United States. Here he provides an insider's perspective on the area and its authentic recipes, like a soup with baby clams and fregula (a toasted semolina pasta that came to Sardinia from North Africa) and pork ribs served with lentils and saba (a tangy-sweet syrup). Sardinian cuisine—a blend of Roman, Arabian, Catalan and other Mediterranean influences—is a fascinating hybrid, and adventurous cooks will love exploring the new flavors here.

featured recipes Pork Ribs with Lentils & Saba; Soup of Fregula with Baby Clams; Watermelon Salad with Arugula, Ricotta Salata & Walnuts; Vegetable Soup with Fresh Ricotta

best of the best exclusive Artichoke & Clam Risotto

Find more recipes by Efisio Farris at foodandwine.com/farris.

PORK RIBS WITH LENTILS & SABA
COSTILLIAS DE PORCU KIN LENTIZZA E SAPA

SERVES 4

- 1 pound French green lentils
- 5 cups beef stock
- 4 tablespoons extra-virgin olive oil
- 2 pounds pork ribs, cut into 1-rib pieces
- ½ cup Cannonau wine (or other dry red wine)
- 1 medium onion, julienned
- 3 garlic cloves, cracked
- 6 sprigs thyme, leaves only
- 2 sprigs rosemary
- 6 juniper berries, smashed and finely chopped
- Sea salt and freshly ground black pepper
- ⅓ cup saba

EDITOR'S NOTE
Saba is a thick Italian syrup made by cooking down unfermented grape juice. It is available at some specialty stores and from gourmetsardinia.com.

The slaughter of a pig was a time of celebration, joining friends and family around one of our most primal connections to life and death. Our pig, of course, was not the only pig in town, but one of many that linked friends and family throughout the late fall and early winter. It would take two days to complete the butchering, with the second day reserved for sectioning the carcass and cutting the meat for sausage. The host family would then thank the friends who helped by presenting them with s'ispinu—*three of the ribs with the loin attached.*
The remaining ribs were cut from the loin, and our family ate them one at a time over the next couple of days. You will obviously serve your family more than one today, but you can celebrate the same way we did with this recipe of ribs and lentils, which, along with the juniper, make a fantastic combination.

Soak lentils in fresh water at least 4 hours. Drain.

In a saucepan, warm beef stock over medium heat.

In a Dutch oven, heat olive oil over medium heat. Add ribs and sear on all sides. Pour in wine and let simmer for a few minutes, stirring to release browned bits on the bottom of the pan. Stir in onion, garlic, thyme, rosemary, and juniper berries. Let cook for 5 minutes, stirring often. Stir in 1 cup of warm stock. Reduce heat to medium-low and cook, uncovered, for 20 minutes.

Stir in lentils and remaining 4 cups of stock. Season to taste with salt and pepper. Reduce heat to low and cook for 45 minutes.

Add saba, stir well to incorporate, and simmer for 5 minutes. Remove from heat and let rest a few minutes before serving. Serve ribs atop a bed of the lentils.

SOUP OF FREGULA WITH BABY CLAMS
FREGULA KIN ARSELLAS

SERVES 4

24   littleneck clams or cockles
5   cups fish stock (or vegetable stock)
¼   cup plus 2 tablespoons extra-virgin
     olive oil
2   garlic cloves, thinly sliced
1   small bunch flat-leaf parsley,
     finely chopped
1   pinch crushed red pepper
Sea salt
1½   cups fregula (see Fregula on p. 95)
1   pinch saffron
3   medium Roma tomatoes,
     seeded and diced
Grated zest of 1 lemon

EDITOR'S NOTE

Good-quality frozen fish stock
is sold at many fish markets and
specialty food stores. You can
also substitute equal parts bottled
clam broth and water.

This soup is a Sardinian classic. Everywhere on the island, the small hard-shell clams (arselle) thrive in the sand near the water's edge and always have. When I was young, I loved to dig for them at the beach, purging them in a bucket of salt water and taking them home for my mother to make this clam soup. Today, any Sardinian restaurant has this soup on the menu because all Sardinians know it and anyone can make it—and should. It is a great representative of our cuisine and showcases the versatility of one of our signature pastas, fregula. It is also easy to make once you prep the ingredients. Be sure to buy fresh clams that are already purged of sand and impurities. The soup is best presented in a low, wide soup bowl so the clams can be laid around the edges of the dish.

Wash clams thoroughly with fresh water. Place clams in a large pot with 1 cup of the stock. Heat until clams open. Remove the clams with a slotted spoon and set aside, keeping warm. Pass cooking liquids through a sieve lined with cheesecloth to remove any sediment and impurities and reserve.

Bring remaining stock to a boil in a saucepan.

Heat ¼ cup of olive oil over medium heat in a large pot (terra-cotta if possible). Add sliced garlic, parsley, and crushed red pepper and sauté until garlic is tender, about 1 minute.

continued on p. 95

SOUP OF FREGULA WITH BABY CLAMS

Add the reserved clam juice mixture and boiling stock. Add salt to taste (carefully, since the natural clam juice is already salty). Bring to a boil, add fregula, saffron, and tomatoes and cook 10 minutes on medium heat. Stir frequently to prevent sticking. (Add more stock if broth seems dry.)

Remove pot from heat and stir in lemon zest. Divide clams among bowls, placing clams around rim. Fill with the soup. Drizzle with remaining olive oil.

FREGULA Fregula—small, toasted semolina pasta—comes to Sardinia from the North African cuisine of the Maghreb. The Ligurians imported fregula from Tabarka (now part of Tunisia) through the Sardinian island of San Pietro, and it remains one of the few Moorish ingredients in our traditional cuisine. The name comes from the Latin word *fricare,* which means "to crumble," and that's what it looks like: crumbled bits of handmade pasta that bear some resemblance to Israeli couscous. In Orosei, we called fregula *su ministru* (little pieces), which we used in soups. I remember Mannai Vardeu making it start to finish by hand, her baskets of little grains drying outside on a sunny day. Today, fregula is still mostly handmade the way my friends Pietro and Donatella make it in their shop in the small town of Riola near Oristano. While they use a machine to knead the large quantities of dough and cut it into small pieces, they still complete the process by hand. First, they take the cut pasta and mix it with extra water and flour to give it a rustic coating. The pieces are then sifted through a *setaccio* (sieve), placed on a tray to dry, and toasted twice before they are ready to eat.

WATERMELON SALAD WITH ARUGULA, RICOTTA SALATA & WALNUTS
SINDRIA A ISSALATA

SERVES 4

- 1 large chunk seedless watermelon (about 1 pound)
- 1½ cups coarsely chopped arugula
- 1 small red onion, sliced into thin rings
- 2 tablespoons raspberry vinegar

Juice of 1 lime

Juice of 1 small orange

Sea salt and freshly ground black pepper

- 1 cup chopped walnuts
- 2 ounces coarsely grated ricotta salata

1 to 2 tablespoons extra-virgin olive oil

This salad is a natural combination for me: in Orosei, bitter greens like arugula and dandelion grow alongside watermelons. Every summer, my brothers and I walked to the river to pick watermelons just as my father had taught us, looking for only the ripest fruit with mature (dry) stems. We piled them proudly by the riverbank and waited for my father to come, watching as he inspected and then tapped each one and listened for the hollow echo that meant they were ripe. Pocketknife at the ready, he then cut a triangle about two inches wide, tasted it, and said the words we loved to hear: "This is beautiful." So is this salad. The refreshing, cool sweetness of the watermelon and creamy ricotta salata is balanced by the peppery bitterness of the arugula and the crunch of red onions and walnuts. Today, I like to enhance this salad of my youth with the sweet/tangy flavor of raspberry vinegar.

Remove the inside of the watermelon and cut into 1-inch cubes. Combine watermelon, arugula and red onion in a large bowl. Refrigerate for 1 hour.

In a separate bowl, mix the raspberry vinegar, lime juice, and orange juice. Refrigerate for 1 hour.

Remove from refrigerator and combine watermelon mixture and vinegar mixture. Season with salt and pepper to taste.

Divide among four plates and drizzle with any dressing that remains in the bowl. Top with the walnuts and ricotta. Finish with a drizzling of olive oil.

VEGETABLE SOUP WITH FRESH RICOTTA
MINESTRONE KIN RECOTTU

SERVES 4

- 4 new potatoes, cubed
- 1 medium zucchini, cubed
- 2 medium carrots, cubed
- 1 stalk celery, sliced
- ½ head green cabbage, cut into 1-inch ribbons
- 1 cup shelled fresh cranberry beans
- 1 teaspoon sea salt
- 2 to 3 tablespoons extra-virgin olive oil
- 1 white onion, diced
- 3 garlic cloves, minced
- ½ pound Roma tomatoes, peeled, seeded, drained, and chopped
- 2 tablespoons tomato paste
- 1 bunch parsley, finely chopped
- 1 cup sheep's milk ricotta cheese (or other creamy ricotta cheese)

EDITOR'S NOTE
Fresh cranberry and other shell beans are sold at farmers' markets in the summer. If they're not available, frozen fava beans are a good stand-in here. Add them during the last 10 minutes of cooking.

My mother and sisters can make this refreshing summer minestrone from memory. I need a little help remembering. But we all learned it from watching Mannai Carta create it in her kitchen. I lived most of my childhood in my grandmother's home, and I remember always having a lot of fun helping her cook and hearing my grandfather's stories. When we made this soup, my job was shelling the beans my grandfather brought in fresh from the fields. In fact, all the ingredients in this family-style soup are fresh; it features staples of Sardinian summer produce as well as fresh, creamy ricotta. I sometimes prefer to eat this soup warm with the cold ricotta; the contrast of temperatures gives the flavors extra brightness.

Place 6 cups of water in a large stock pot. Add potatoes, zucchini, carrots, celery, cabbage, beans, and sea salt and bring to a rolling boil over medium heat. Once mixture begins to boil, reduce heat to low and simmer for 10 to 15 minutes or until vegetables are easily pierced with a fork.

In a saucepan, heat olive oil over medium heat. Add onion and garlic and cook until softened. Add tomatoes, tomato paste, parsley, and a pinch of salt. When mixture begins to bubble, reduce heat to low and let simmer for 10 to 15 minutes, stirring often to prevent sticking.

Add tomato mixture to stock pot and stir to combine. Divide among serving bowls and top each with a spoonful of fresh ricotta.

best of the best exclusive
ARTICHOKE & CLAM RISOTTO

SERVES 4

3¼ cups water
  2 pounds littleneck clams, scrubbed
  1 cup store-bought clam broth
  3 tablespoons extra-virgin olive oil
  2 garlic cloves, smashed
  1 medium shallot, minced
  1 bay leaf
  2 cups arborio rice
  1 cup dry white wine
One 10-ounce box frozen baby artichoke
      quarters, thawed and drained
  2 tablespoons coarsely chopped
      flat-leaf parsley leaves
  2 tablespoons chopped dill
Kosher salt and freshly ground pepper

1. In a large saucepan, bring 1 cup of the water to a boil. Add the clams, cover and cook over moderately high heat until they open, about 4 minutes. With a slotted spoon, transfer the clams to a bowl. Discard any that do not open. Strain the cooking liquid through a fine strainer into a medium saucepan. Add the remaining 2¼ cups of water and the clam broth and bring to a simmer over moderately high heat. Reduce the heat to low and keep warm. Remove the clams from their shells; discard the shells.

2. In a large saucepan, heat the olive oil. Add the garlic cloves and cook over moderate heat until light golden, about 4 minutes, then remove and discard them. Add the shallot and bay leaf and cook over moderate heat until the shallot is softened, about 2 minutes. Add the rice and cook, stirring, until the rice is well coated with oil, about 30 seconds. Add the wine and cook, stirring constantly, until absorbed, about 2 minutes. Add ½ cup of the hot clam stock and cook, stirring, until absorbed. Continue adding the stock ½ cup at a time and stirring constantly until it is absorbed before adding more. The risotto is done when the rice is just tender and suspended in creamy liquid, about 20 minutes. Discard the bay leaf. Fold the clams, artichokes, parsley and dill into the risotto and season with salt and pepper. Spoon the risotto into warmed bowls and serve.

Casas investigates both classic and modern tapas.

TAPAS

PENELOPE CASAS

PUBLISHED BY ALFRED A. KNOPF, $30

Penelope Casas originally published this book more than 20 years ago, before most Americans had ever heard of tapas. Now, of course, tapas are ubiquitous, and Casas has completely revised and updated her seminal volume, adding over 50 new recipes. An American who splits her time between the United States and Spain, Casas looks at the way tapas culture has changed in the past two decades, then presents the best tapas—both traditional and innovative—in Spain today. Two standouts: the Pork Ribs in Paprika Sauce from Bar Bahía in Cádiz, and Casas's own recipe for Fried Cheese with Shallot Dressing. With this book, Casas has reinvigorated a kind of cooking and eating that is in danger of becoming too trendy for its own good.

featured recipes Mortadella & Ham Salad; Pork Ribs in Paprika Sauce; Green Olive "Pâté" Canapé; Fried Cheese with Shallot Dressing

best of the best exclusive Butter Beans & Smoked Fish in Caper Vinaigrette

Find more recipes by Penelope Casas at foodandwine.com/casas.

MORTADELLA & HAM SALAD
ENSALADA DE MORTADELA Y JAMÓN

SERVES 6

- ¼ pound mortadella, cut in thin slices, then in 2-inch-long julienne strips
- ¼ pound boiled ham, cut in thin slices, then in 2-inch-long julienne strips
- 2 *piquillo* peppers
- 4 tablespoons minced dill or cornichon pickle
- ½ cup minced onion, preferably Vidalia or other sweet onion
- 2 tablespoons minced parsley

DRESSING

- ¼ cup extra-virgin olive oil
- 2 tablespoons red wine vinegar
- ¼ teaspoon Dijon-style mustard
- Kosher or sea salt
- Freshly ground pepper

EDITOR'S NOTE

Mortadella is a large, soft, smoked sausage made of seasoned beef and pork and studded with cubed pork fat. Originally from Bologna, Italy, it was the inspiration for American bologna, a.k.a. baloney. Look for imported mortadella at Italian specialty stores and good deli counters.

I have sampled two versions of this salad, one with a vinaigrette dressing and the other with salsa rosada—*mayonnaise and tomato. Although I prefer the viniagrette, which is slightly tart, family and friends who have sampled both seem to like the sweetness of the other version. This salad may be served right away, but I think it gains in flavor when left to marinate overnight. The main recipe is for the vinaigrette version.*

Prepare one day in advance.

In a bowl mix together the mortadella, ham, *piquillo* peppers, pickle, onion, and parsley. In a small bowl whisk the dressing ingredients, then fold gently into the mortadella mixture. Serve immediately or let marinate for several hours at room temperature, or longer in the refrigerator.

VARIATION Omit the onion and add 1 small carrot, scraped, cut in 1-inch-long julienne strips. Reduce the pickle to 2 tablespoons. Fold in ¼ cup mayonnaise blended with 2 tablespoons ketchup, salt, pepper, and a dash of Worcestershire sauce.

PORK RIBS IN PAPRIKA SAUCE
COSTILLAS BAR BAHÍA

SERVES 4

  1 tablespoon olive oil
1¾ pounds lean pork spare ribs,
     smallest available, cut into
     individual ribs and each rib cut
     crosswise into 1½- to 2-inch pieces
Freshly ground pepper
  2 teaspoons dried oregano
  2 teaspoons sweet paprika,
     preferably Spanish smoked
  1 bay leaf
  1 cup dry white wine
  8 cloves garlic, peeled and crushed
Kosher or sea salt
  1 cup water

EDITOR'S NOTE
Cutting ribs into little riblets takes
some serious chopping with a
good cleaver. We recommend you
ask your butcher to do this.

There is a small, unprepossessing bar, Bar Bahía, on Cádiz's waterfront, where the city's residents know they can find excellent tapas and fine company. Salvador, the bar's lively owner, seems to spend as much time in front of the counter, joking with his customers, as behind the counter, tending to his simmering pots. But when a guest comes from New York, his enthusiasm knows no bounds, and drinks and tapas are often on the house ("We don't have a cent in Cádiz, but what the hell!"). Here is Salvador's recipe for tasty ribs, Cádiz style.

Combine all ingredients except salt and water in a deep cooking casserole. Marinate 1 hour. Add the salt and water, bring to a boil, then lower the heat and cook slowly, covered, for 1 hour or until the ribs are tender. Uncover and boil down the liquid until just a small amount remains to coat the ribs.

GREEN OLIVE "PÂTÉ" CANAPÉ
CANAPÉ DE PASTA DE ACEITUNA VERDE

SERVES 4 (MAKES ABOUT 12)

40   pitted green Spanish olives, coarsely chopped
1   teaspoon capers
4   anchovies, preferably Spanish bottled, coarsely chopped
1   teaspoon finely ground blanched almonds
1   clove garlic, mashed to a paste or put through a garlic press
4   tablespoons fruity extra-virgin olive oil
⅛   teaspoon ground cumin
¼   teaspoon sweet paprika, preferably Spanish smoked
1½   teaspoons fresh thyme, or ¼ teaspoon dried
Freshly ground pepper
About twelve ¼-inch bread rounds cut from a long crusty loaf
Piquillo peppers for garnish

Olives, capers, anchovies, almonds, and garlic, the ingredients in this recipe, are the very essence of the flavor of Spain. This canapé always reminds me of the endless olive groves of Jaén, the plains of Castilla, the taverns of Madrid, Sevilla . . .

The paste is wonderful spread on a slice of bread, but it could also serve as a condiment, enlivening the taste of, for example, meatballs, empanadilla *fillings, and salad dressings.*

Place all ingredients except bread and *piquillo* peppers in the bowl of a processor and mix until as finely chopped as possible. Transfer to a mortar and pound until the mixture forms a paste. [May be prepared ahead.] Spread very thinly on the bread and garnish with pieces of *piquillo*.

The backdrop at
a Basque tapas bar.

FRIED CHEESE WITH SHALLOT DRESSING
QUESO FRITO ALIÑADO CON SALSA DE ESCALONA

SERVES 6

DRESSING

2	tablespoons olive oil
2	teaspoons vinegar
4	teaspoons minced shallots
2	teaspoons minced parsley
½	teaspoon small whole nonpareil or chopped large capers

½	pound fairly mild melting cheese, such as Spanish Tetilla, Mahón, or goat cheese, ½ inch thick, then cut in 1-inch squares

Flour for dusting

2	eggs, lightly beaten with 2 teaspoons water

Dried bread crumbs, preferably mixed with Japanese-style panko crumbs

Mild olive oil for frying

EDITOR'S NOTE

The cheese for this dish should be chilled when you fry it. If you plan to bread the squares in advance, keep them in the refrigerator, uncovered, for up to 6 hours.

Make this tapa even more delicious with one of the exciting soft Spanish cheeses now available in America.

In a cup, combine the dressing ingredients. Dust the cheese pieces with flour, dip in the egg, then in the crumbs. [May be prepared ahead.] In a skillet heat the oil at least ½ inch deep to about 365°F and fry the cheese quickly until golden on both sides. Or, better, use a deep fryer. Drain.

Sprinkle the dressing over the cheese and serve immediately.

best of the best exclusive

BUTTER BEANS & SMOKED FISH IN CAPER VINAIGRETTE

SERVES 4

- 3 tablespoons extra-virgin olive oil
- 1 tablespoon white wine vinegar
- ⅛ teaspoon sugar

Kosher salt and freshly ground pepper

One 15-ounce can butter beans, drained and rinsed

- 1 ounce thinly sliced smoked salmon, cut crosswise into ½-inch ribbons
- 1 ounce skinless smoked trout, cut into ½-inch dice
- 1½ tablespoons finely chopped onion
- 1 tablespoon minced parsley leaves
- 2 teaspoons capers
- 1 teaspoon minced dill

Grilled bread, for serving

EDITOR'S NOTE

This is a fun idea for a tapa because it combines two different kinds of smoked fish with big, hearty butter beans. The dish can also be prepared completely ahead of time, which makes it great for a party.

In a medium bowl, whisk the olive oil with the vinegar and sugar and season with salt and pepper. Add the butter beans, smoked salmon, smoked trout, onion, parsley, capers and dill and toss to coat. Let stand at room temperature for 1 hour. Serve with grilled bread.

MAKE AHEAD This recipe can be refrigerated for up to 1 day. Bring to room temperature before serving.

Anissa Helou (here in her home kitchen) gathered recipes from bakers throughout the Mediterranean, from Morocco to Syria, Turkey to Spain.

SAVORY BAKING FROM THE MEDITERRANEAN

ANISSA HELOU

PUBLISHED BY WILLIAM MORROW, $29.95

There are innumerable books on Mediterranean cooking, but the focus here, on savory baking—flatbreads, focaccias, pizzas, tarts—is singular. So is Anissa Helou, the Lebanese-Syrian author of four Mediterranean cookbooks who has her own cooking school in London. Helou has a talent for writing great recipes that work perfectly and that are full of unconventional ideas; instead of punching down rising bread dough, for example, she recommends folding it. Her supremely light and flaky cheese focaccia from Italy's Ligurian coast and her zesty eggplant "pizza" from Turkey represent Mediterranean baking at its best.

featured recipes Cheese Focaccia from Recco; Eggplant "Pizza"; Moroccan Multilayered Breads; Cheese & Ham Brioche Ring

best of the best exclusive Fava Beans with Swiss Chard & Cilantro

Find more recipes by Anissa Helou at foodandwine.com/helou.

CHEESE FOCACCIA FROM RECCO
FOCACCIA DI FORMAGGIO DI RECCO

SERVES 4

1⅓ cups unbleached all-purpose flour,
  plus extra for kneading and shaping
¾ teaspoon fine kosher salt or sea salt
3 tablespoons extra-virgin olive oil,
  plus extra for brushing the pan and
  the focaccia
9 ounces taleggio, trimmed of skin,
  thinly sliced
Coarse sea salt

In Recco, a small city on the Ligurian coast in Northern Italy, this focaccia is made with a local cheese called formagetta *or* formaggio ligure. *But a soft cow's-milk cheese such as taleggio will work very well. Although this is an unleavened focaccia, it bubbles up beautifully when it bakes and has a light, flaky texture.*

1. Combine the 1⅓ cups flour and the fine salt in a large bowl and make a well in the center. Add the 3 tablespoons oil to the well and, with fingertips, incorporate the oil into the flour completely. Gradually add ⅓ cup plus ½ tablespoon warm water. Knead briefly to make a rough ball of dough.

2. Dust the work surface with flour and knead the dough for 2 to 3 minutes. Invert the bowl over the dough and let rest for 15 minutes. Knead for 2 to 3 minutes more, until the dough is smooth and elastic. Shape the dough into a ball and place it in a lightly floured clean bowl. Cover with plastic wrap and let ferment in a warm, draft-free place for 1 hour. Fold the dough, cover again, and let ferment for 1 hour more. The dough should have doubled in volume.

3. Return the dough to the work surface, divide it in half equally, and shape each half into a ball. Cover both balls with a damp kitchen towel and let rest for 15 minutes.

EDITOR'S NOTE

Let the bread rest for just 5 minutes, then cut it into wedges (a pizza cutter works well for this)—if you slice the focaccia as soon as it comes out of the oven, the cheese will ooze out. Any cheese that melts well will be good here, especially fontina and Gruyère.

4. Dust the work surface with flour. Roll out one piece of dough very thin to a diameter of at least 12 inches, sprinkling with flour every now and then so that it does not stick. Generously brush with olive oil a large nonstick baking sheet, or a baking sheet lined with parchment paper or a silicone pastry mat, and transfer the rolled-out dough to the sheet. Preheat the oven to 500°F.

5. Place the cheese slices evenly over the dough, leaving ½ inch free at the edges. Roll out the other piece of dough to the same diameter as the first and place this layer over the cheese. Press on the edges to seal. Brush liberally with olive oil and let rest while the oven is preheating.

6. Press with fingertips on the focaccia to make dimples all over. Sprinkle with coarse salt. Bake for 8 to 10 minutes, or until golden brown all over. Serve hot, while the cheese is still melted.

EGGPLANT "PIZZA"
PATLICANLI PIDE

SERVES 4

FOR THE DOUGH
- ¾ teaspoon (⅓ package) active dry yeast
- 1¾ cups unbleached all-purpose flour, plus extra for kneading and shaping
- 1 teaspoon fine kosher salt or sea salt
- 2 tablespoons extra-virgin olive oil

FOR THE TOPPING
- 3 tablespoons extra-virgin olive oil, plus extra to drizzle over the breads
- 1 medium eggplant (about ½ pound), cut into small cubes
- ½ red bell pepper, cored, seeded, and finely chopped
- Kosher salt or sea salt
- Freshly ground black pepper
- 1 garlic clove, crushed
- 7 to 8 ounces canned peeled tomatoes, drained
- ⅛ teaspoon red pepper flakes, or to taste
- ¼ cup finely chopped flat-leaf parsley
- ¼ cup finely chopped cilantro

Fresh basil leaves, for garnish

Turkish cooks use a variety of toppings for their version of pizza, including greens, eggs, cheese, spicy sausage, and meats. I have adapted this recipe from one in Ayla Algar's Classic Turkish Cookery. I first made it for my friend Jeremy Lee, the wonderful chef at the Blueprint Café in London, who liked the breads so much he asked for the recipe so that he could have them on his menu. I am not normally mean-spirited, but I showed a remarkable lack of generosity by refusing to share the recipe with him. Ever since, we have had a running joke about when I would give him the recipe for the eggplant breads. I almost relented once or twice, but I decided to wait until this book was published. And now that this book is in print, he can finally have patlicanli pide on his menu.

1. MAKE THE DOUGH Dissolve the yeast in ½ cup warm water and stir until creamy. Combine the flour and salt in a large bowl and make a well in the center. Add the olive oil to the well and, with fingertips, rub it into the flour until well incorporated. Add the yeast and mix until you have a rough ball of dough.

2. Remove the dough to a lightly floured work surface. Knead for 3 minutes. Invert the bowl over the dough and let rest for 15 minutes. Knead for 2 to 3 minutes more, until the dough is smooth and elastic. Cover with a wet but not dripping kitchen towel and let rise in a warm, draft-free place for 30 minutes.

3. MEANWHILE, MAKE THE TOPPING Put the olive oil, eggplant, and bell pepper in a sauté pan over low heat. Season with salt and pepper to taste. Cook, covered, for 15 minutes, stirring frequently. Add the garlic, tomatoes, and pepper flakes and cook, covered, for 15 minutes more, stirring occasionally and breaking up the tomatoes, until the vegetables are cooked through and the sauce is very thick. Add the parsley and cilantro and cook, uncovered, for another minute. Remove from the heat, cover with a kitchen towel, and let cool.

4. Preheat the oven to 400°F. Return the dough to the work surface and divide it into 4 equal pieces. Shape each into a ball, cover with a damp kitchen towel, and let rest for 15 minutes. Flatten each ball by hand into a circle about 5 inches in diameter, then stretch the circles into ovals and flatten further. Transfer to a large nonstick baking sheet, or to a baking sheet lined with parchment paper or a silicone pastry mat. Make indentations with fingertips inside the edges of the ovals to raise them slightly. Spread one-quarter of the topping inside the raised edges of each pizza.

5. Bake for 10 to 15 minutes, until the crust is golden. Garnish with basil leaves and serve hot or warm.

MOROCCAN MULTILAYERED BREADS
R'GHAYEF

MAKES 8 INDIVIDUAL BREADS

FOR THE DOUGH
- ½ teaspoon (scant ¼ package) active dry yeast
- 1 cup unbleached all-purpose flour, plus extra for kneading
- 1 cup semolina flour
- 1 teaspoon fine kosher salt or sea salt

FOR THE FILLING
- 1 medium onion, very finely chopped
- ¼ cup finely chopped flat-leaf parsley
- ½ teaspoon ground cumin
- 1 teaspoon sweet paprika
- ⅛ teaspoon crushed red pepper flakes

Kosher salt or sea salt

Vegetable oil

You find r'ghayef, *with slight variations, in Tunisia and Algeria as well as in Morocco. In Algeria, the breads are known as* m'hajjib *and in Tunisia as* m'lawi. *In Tunisia, plain* m'lawi *are used as wraps to make sandwiches.* R'ghayef *are also called* m'semmen *in Morocco. There is a recipe for a similar bread,* musammana *(which means "buttered"), in a thirteenth-century cookbook from across the sea in Andalucia.*

1. Dissolve the yeast in ⅔ cup plus 2 tablespoons warm water and stir until creamy.

2. Combine the flours and salt in a large bowl and make a well in the center. Add the yeast and mix with the flour until you have a rough, sticky dough.

3. Remove the dough to a lightly floured work surface. Sprinkle the dough with flour and knead for about 3 minutes. Invert the bowl over the dough and let rest for 15 minutes. Knead for about 2 to 3 minutes more, until the dough is smooth and elastic. Cover with a damp kitchen towel and let rest while the filling is prepared.

4. Combine the filling ingredients in a medium bowl. Mix well.

EDITOR'S NOTE
These folded, stuffed breads
are a great alternative to pita for
a Middle Eastern–style meal.
Feel free to vary the filling to
taste; you can use 1½ teaspoons
of curry powder in place of the
spices called for, or add chopped
mushrooms along with the onion.

5. Divide the dough into 8 equal pieces. Oil a work surface and your hands. Flatten a ball by hand on the work surface into a very thin circle using more oil if necessary. Spread one-eighth of the filling over the center of the circle. Fold the left third of the circle over the filling, then fold the right third over to make a rectangle. Fold the top third over the bread and the bottom third under the bread to make a square about 5 inches on each side; folding one side up and the other down encloses the filling evenly and securely. Let rest while you make 3 more squares in the same manner (the last 4 breads will be made in a second batch). Flatten with fingertips the squares of filled dough until they are quite thin.

6. Oil a large nonstick frying pan and place over medium-high heat. Place 1 or 2 squares in the hot pan. Drizzle a little additional oil over the bread. Cook for 1½ to 2 minutes on each side, until golden. Remove to parchment paper or a wire rack. Cook the remaining 2 or 3 breads from this first batch, then shape, fill, and cook the remaining 4 breads, using plenty of oil as needed for work surface, hands, and pan. Serve immediately.

Many Mediterranean doughs are made by mounding flour on a work surface, creating an indentation in the center, then pouring in eggs and mixing.

CHEESE & HAM BRIOCHE RING
LA CIAMBELLA DI BRIOSCIA

SERVES 6 TO 8

4½ teaspoons (2 packages) active
   dry yeast
3 cups plus 1 tablespoon unbleached
   all-purpose flour
¾ teaspoon fine kosher salt or sea salt
4 tablespoons (½ stick) unsalted
   butter, melted, plus extra butter
   for greasing the ring mold and
   plastic wrap
3 large eggs
½ cup lukewarm milk
½ teaspoon freshly ground
   black pepper
1½ cups freshly grated Parmigiano-
   Reggiano (about 3 ounces)
1 cup coarsely grated provolone
   (about 2 ounces)
3 ounces ham, cut into short,
   thin strips

This is an impressive creation, which in Italy often is served hot with sliced red and yellow peppers sautéed in olive oil, garnished with chopped parsley and capers and seasoned with a little vinegar. The peppers are piled inside the ring of bread and the whole thing is served as a starter. It's also good at room temperature with a simple green salad and a selection of salami and cheeses. The ciambella keeps well for several days and makes a great snack, sliced and toasted.

1. Dissolve the yeast in ¾ cup warm water in a medium bowl and stir until creamy. Add 1 cup of the flour and ¼ teaspoon of the salt and mix with a rubber spatula to make a thick, rough batter. Sprinkle 1 tablespoon flour over the top. Cover with plastic wrap and let rise in a warm, draft-free place for 1 hour. This will be the sponge, or biga.

2. Put the melted butter in a large bowl. Stir in the eggs, one at a time. Add the sponge and mix, using a whisk, until all the ingredients are well blended.

3. Gradually add the remaining 2 cups flour, adding the milk between additions and mixing with a rubber spatula to make a smooth, thick batter. Cover with plastic wrap and let rise in a warm, draft-free place for 1 hour, until doubled in volume.

continued on p. 118

4. Use about 2 tablespoons of the extra unsalted butter to generously butter a large ring mold. Add the remaining salt and the pepper to the batter together with the grated cheeses and the ham. Mix with a spatula until all the ingredients are evenly incorporated.

5. Pour the mixture into the ring mold, lightly pressing on it with the back of a spoon to distribute it evenly and to break up air pockets. Cover with a buttered piece of plastic wrap and then with a heavy kitchen towel. Let rise for about 1 hour. The batter should have doubled in volume. Meanwhile, preheat the oven to 375°F.

6. Uncover the bread and bake for 25 to 30 minutes, until well risen and golden all over. Remove the mold to a wire rack. Let sit for about 15 minutes, then unmold the bread onto the rack to cool. Serve at room temperature.

best of the best exclusive

FAVA BEANS WITH
SWISS CHARD & CILANTRO

SERVES 6

¼ cup extra-virgin olive oil
2 onions, finely chopped
4 garlic cloves, smashed
2 bunches of Swiss chard (1¾ pounds), stalks cut into ½-inch dice, leaves cut into ½-inch-wide ribbons
3 cups cilantro leaves (from 1 medium bunch), coarsely chopped
½ pound frozen shelled fava beans, thawed (see Note)
3 tablespoons fresh lemon juice
Kosher salt
Warm pita, for serving

EDITOR'S NOTE
Helou found this recipe, a specialty of Beirut's large Sunni Muslim community, in a friend's family cookbook, which noted that spinach could be used in place of the chard. The dish can be served as part of a meze spread, as a side or as a vegetarian main course.

In a large pot, heat the olive oil. Add the onions and cook over moderate heat until softened, about 8 minutes. Add the garlic and cook until fragrant, about 1 minute. Add the Swiss chard stalks, cover and cook over low heat until tender, about 20 minutes. Add the Swiss chard leaves and the cilantro, cover and cook until the greens are softened, about 15 minutes. Stir in the fava beans and lemon juice and season with salt. Cook uncovered over moderate heat until the greens are tender and the juices are thickened, about 15 minutes. Remove from the heat and let stand until cool, about 30 minutes. Serve at room temperature with warm pita.

NOTE Frozen shelled fava beans can be found in many large supermarkets or health-food stores.

MAKE AHEAD This dish can be refrigerated for up to 2 days. Bring to room temperature before serving.

ASIAN

SICHUAN BOILED DUMPLINGS
WITH SPICY DIPPING SAUCE, P. 124

THE SHUN LEE COOKBOOK

MICHAEL TONG & ELAINE LOUIE

PUBLISHED BY WILLIAM MORROW, $29.95

Michael Tong, the restaurateur behind New York City's Shun Lee, played a pivotal role in introducing Americans to the varied regional cuisines of China (from Sichuan, Hunan and Shanghai) back in the 1960s. Today, almost every Chinese restaurant in the United States serves the dishes Shun Lee debuted over 40 years ago, like cold sesame noodles and chicken chow fun. Very few cookbooks, however, offer recipes as good as these. In adapting his restaurant recipes for the home kitchen, Tong took pains to make sure they would work, with remarkable success. And the dishes are absolutely delicious, from the Crispy Orange Beef to the Twice-Cooked Pork.

featured recipes Sichuan Boiled Dumplings with Spicy Dipping Sauce; Crispy Orange Beef; Hunan Lamb with Scallions; Twice-Cooked Pork

best of the best exclusive Braised Whole Sea Bass with Pork & Garlic

SICHUAN BOILED DUMPLINGS WITH SPICY DIPPING SAUCE

MAKES 20 DUMPLINGS, OR 4 SERVINGS

FILLING

- 8 ounces ground pork
- 2 ounces small shrimp, peeled, deveined, and minced
- 1 tablespoon soy sauce
- 1 tablespoon vegetable oil
- 1 tablespoon minced cilantro
- 1 scallion, green and white parts, trimmed and minced
- 1 Chinese dried black mushroom, soaked until softened, stem trimmed, and cap minced
- 1 teaspoon dark sesame oil
- ¼ teaspoon ground white pepper

- 2 tablespoons cornstarch, plus more for sprinkling

About 20 round dumpling wrappers

SAUCE

- 2 tablespoons vegetable oil
- 2 scallions, white part only, trimmed and minced
- 5 garlic cloves, peeled and minced
- 1 tablespoon freshly ground black pepper
- 2 tablespoons sugar
- 2 tablespoons Chinese black vinegar or balsamic vinegar
- 2 tablespoons hot bean paste
- 1 tablespoon soy sauce
- 1 tablespoon dark sesame oil
- 1 tablespoon hot chile oil

Fried dumplings have legions of fans, but there is something soulfully satisfying about the simplicity of their boiled cousins. What gives character to these boiled dumplings is the wonderful dipping sauce, seasoned with spicy sesame oil.

1. For the filling, combine the pork, shrimp, soy sauce, vegetable oil, cilantro, scallion, mushroom, sesame oil, white pepper, and ⅓ cup water in a medium bowl. Mix well. Cover, and freeze for 1 hour (or refrigerate overnight) to firm the mixture and make it easier to handle.

2. Dissolve the cornstarch in 3 tablespoons cold water in a small bowl to make a paste. Line a baking sheet with waxed paper and sprinkle it with cornstarch. Moisten the edges of a dumpling wrapper by dipping your finger into the paste and running it over the edge of the wrapper. Using a blunt knife as a scoop, place about a tablespoon of the filling in the center of the wrapper. Bring the edges of the wrapper up to meet at the top of the filling and pinch them closed, squeezing the dough. Place the dumpling on the baking sheet. Repeat with the remaining filling and wrappers. (The uncooked dumplings can be made ahead, covered with plastic wrap, and refrigerated for up to 1 day. Or freeze them for up to 3 months. To freeze, place them in a single layer in a plastic storage container or plastic storage bag, arranged so that the dumplings don't touch one another. When you are ready to cook them, the frozen dumplings will be easy to remove, one by one.)

EDITOR'S NOTE

Hot bean paste is a savory, spicy combination of fermented soybeans and chiles. Look for jars at Asian markets.

3. Bring a large saucepan of water to a boil over high heat. Add the dumplings and cover the pan. Cook until the filling is cooked through and the dumplings are floating on top of the water, about 4 minutes.

4. While the dumplings are cooking, make the sauce: Heat a wok or medium skillet over high heat. Add the oil and heat until it shimmers. Add the scallions, garlic, and black pepper, and stir-fry for 20 seconds. Transfer to a small bowl. Add the sugar, vinegar, hot bean paste, soy sauce, sesame oil, and hot chile oil to the scallions, and mix well. Divide the sauce among four soup bowls.

5. Carefully drain the dumplings in a colander. Place the dumplings on top of the sauce in the bowls, and serve immediately.

CRISPY ORANGE BEEF

SERVES 4

8 ounces flank steak, cut into
  pieces 1 inch long, ½ inch wide,
  and ¼ inch thick
1½ teaspoons baking soda
1 orange

SAUCE
2 tablespoons sugar
2 tablespoons red wine vinegar
1 tablespoon rice wine
  or dry sherry
1 tablespoon soy sauce
1 teaspoon cornstarch

Vegetable oil, for passing through
1 cup cornstarch
1 large egg white, lightly beaten
3 scallions, white part only, trimmed
  and sliced diagonally into ½-inch
  pieces (½ cup)
1 teaspoon dark sesame oil
1 tablespoon orange liqueur, such as
  Grand Marnier
¼ teaspoon hot chile paste

The original Sichuan recipe for this dish was for a cold, somewhat chewy appetizer of fried, dried, and shredded beef. It is a far cry from Shun Lee's Crispy Orange Beef, which was introduced in 1971, and which millions of Americans have since come to love.

1. Mix the flank steak, baking soda, and 3 tablespoons of water in a medium bowl. Cover, and refrigerate for 4 hours or overnight. (The baking soda will tenderize the steak.)

2. Using a vegetable peeler, remove the colored zest from the orange. Cut the zest into thin strips about 1 inch long, and set them aside. Save the orange flesh for another use.

3. To begin the sauce, mix the sugar, vinegar, rice wine, soy sauce, and cornstarch in a small bowl. Set it aside.

4. Heat a large wok over high heat. Add enough vegetable oil to come about 1½ inches up the sides of the wok, and heat it to 375°F. Meanwhile, add the cornstarch and egg white to the steak, and mix well to coat the steak with the batter.

5. Add the flank steak to the oil, one piece at a time so it doesn't splash or stick together, and stir gently until it begins to look crispy, about 1 minute. Using a wide wire-mesh strainer, transfer the steak to a colander to drain. Using a fine-mesh wire strainer, remove any bits of fried batter from the wok.

EDITOR'S NOTE
To cut raw meat superthin for stir-frying, freeze it for 30 minutes to 1 hour before slicing. You'll be able to create thin, uniform pieces of beef for this addictive recipe.

6. Reheat the oil to 375°F, return the flank steak to the wok, and fry again until the beef is crispy all over, about 2 minutes. Transfer to a strainer to drain. Discard all but 1 tablespoon of the oil from the wok.

7. Return the wok with the oil to high heat. Add the scallions, flank steak, sugar-vinegar mixture, orange zest, sesame oil, Grand Marnier, and hot chile paste. Stir-fry until all of the ingredients are well-blended, about 30 seconds. Serve immediately.

HUNAN LAMB WITH SCALLIONS

SERVES 4

- 1 pound boneless leg of lamb, trimmed
- 1 large egg
- 1½ tablespoons cornstarch

Vegetable oil, for passing through

- ¼ cup canned sliced bamboo shoots (cut into thin 1½-inch-long strips)

SAUCE

- 3 tablespoons rice wine or dry sherry
- 2 tablespoons soy sauce
- 2 tablespoons sugar
- 2 tablespoons distilled white vinegar
- 1 tablespoon hot bean paste

Pinch of ground white pepper

- 1½ teaspoons cornstarch

- 1 leek, white part only, trimmed and cut into thin 1½-inch-long strips, well washed
- 5 garlic cloves, peeled and sliced ⅛ inch thick
- 4 scallions, white and green parts, trimmed and sliced diagonally into ¼-inch pieces

Shun Lee introduced lamb to its menu in 1972, and since then other Chinese restaurants have followed suit. Here, tender slices of meat from the lamb leg are bound with scallions and leeks in a spicy, garlicky sauce.

1. Cut the lamb across the grain into ¼-inch-thick slices. Cut the slices into pieces about 2 inches long and 1 inch wide. Mix the lamb with the egg, cornstarch, and 1 tablespoon water in a medium bowl. Cover, and refrigerate for 30 minutes.

2. Heat a large wok over high heat. Add enough oil to come about 1 inch up the sides of the wok, and heat it to 325°F. Add the lamb carefully, so the pieces don't splash or stick to each other, and stir gently until they turn light brown, about 30 seconds. Add the bamboo shoots and stir for 20 seconds. Using a wide wire-mesh strainer, transfer the lamb and bamboo shoots to a colander to drain. Discard all but 2 tablespoons of the oil from the wok.

continued on p. 130

3. To begin the sauce, mix the rice wine, soy sauce, sugar, vinegar, hot bean paste, and white pepper in a small bowl, and set it aside. Dissolve the cornstarch in 2 tablespoons cold water in another small bowl, and set it aside.

4. Return the wok with the oil to high heat. Add the leek and garlic, and stir-fry until the garlic is fragrant, about 15 seconds. Return the lamb and bamboo shoots to the wok; then add the scallions and the rice wine mixture, and stir-fry for 10 seconds. Add the cornstarch mixture and stir-fry until the lamb turns a dark brown and the sauce has evenly coated the meat and vegetables, about 20 seconds. Serve immediately.

TWICE-COOKED PORK

SERVES 4

10 ounces boneless pork butt
6 ounces (8 leaves) Napa cabbage, cut into pieces 2 inches long and 1½ inches wide
Vegetable oil, for passing through

SAUCE
2 tablespoons hoisin sauce
2 tablespoons soy sauce
2 tablespoons rice wine or dry sherry
1 tablespoon sugar
1 tablespoon distilled white vinegar
2 teaspoons hot bean paste
1 teaspoon cornstarch

2 scallions, white part only, trimmed and sliced diagonally into ½-inch pieces
1 leek, white part only, trimmed and cut into thin 1½-inch-long strips, well washed
3 garlic cloves, peeled and sliced ⅛ inch thick
1 small hot fresh chile, such as Thai or serrano, seeds and ribs removed, cut into thin 1½-inch-long strips
2 teaspoons hot chile oil, optional
1 teaspoon dark sesame oil

In the authentic Sichuan version of this dish, pork belly is boiled, sliced, and fried, but lean pork butt works, too. This rendition, inspired by the flavors of Shanghai, has a touch of sweetness from hoisin sauce.

1. Bring 4 cups of water to a boil in a medium saucepan over high heat. Add the pork and return to a boil. Reduce the heat to medium-low and simmer, uncovered, until the pork is about 85 percent cooked (when sliced, it should have a pale pink center), about 15 minutes. Transfer the pork to a cutting board and let it cool. Then cut it crosswise into ⅛-inch-thick slices, and cut the slices into pieces about 1½ inches long and 1 inch wide.

2. Return the saucepan of the pork-cooking water to high heat. Add 2 more cups of water and bring to a boil. Add the cabbage and cook for 2 minutes. Drain the cabbage in a colander.

3. Heat a large wok over high heat. Add enough vegetable oil to come about 1½ inches up the sides of the wok, and heat it to 300°F. Add the pork and stir gently until it is pale beige, about 20 seconds. Using a wide wire-mesh strainer, transfer the pork to a colander to drain. Discard all but 3 tablespoons of the oil from the wok.

continued on p. 133

TWICE-COOKED PORK

EDITOR'S NOTE

The recipe makes plenty of sauce, so you can use twice as much cabbage if you want this stir-fry heavy on vegetables.

4. To begin the sauce, combine the hoisin sauce, soy sauce, rice wine, sugar, vinegar, and hot bean paste in a small bowl, and set it aside. Dissolve the cornstarch in 1 tablespoon cold water, and set it aside.

5. Return the wok with the oil to high heat. Add the scallions, leek, garlic, and chile, and stir-fry for 20 seconds. Return the pork and cabbage to the wok, and add the hoisin sauce mixture and the cornstarch mixture. Stir-fry until the sauce comes to a boil and thickens, about 20 seconds. Add the hot chile oil if using, and then the sesame oil. Serve immediately.

best of the best exclusive

BRAISED WHOLE SEA BASS WITH PORK & GARLIC

SERVES 2

One 2-pound sea bass, cleaned
- ¼ cup plus 1 teaspoon soy sauce
- 2 cups vegetable oil
- 24 garlic cloves, peeled
- ¼ pound pork tenderloin, sliced ⅛ inch thick

One 2-inch piece of ginger, peeled and cut into 2-by-⅛-inch matchsticks
- 2 cups water
- ¼ cup dry sherry
- ¼ cup sugar
- 1 tablespoon cornstarch mixed with 2 tablespoons water
- 1 teaspoon Asian sesame oil
- 6 cilantro sprigs
- 1 scallion, thinly sliced lengthwise and cut into 2-inch lengths

EDITOR'S NOTE

Frying a whole fish is a little tricky. If you prefer, you can simply skip this step—the fish will cook through in the tasty sauce in Step 3.

1. Using a sharp knife, cut 5 evenly spaced slits on each side of the fish. Rub the fish with 1 teaspoon of the soy sauce. Let stand for 10 minutes, then pat the fish dry.

2. In a large wok or very large, deep skillet, heat the oil until it registers 350°F on a deep-fry thermometer. Gently slide the fish into the hot oil and fry over moderately high heat, turning once, until the skin begins to turn light golden, about 1 minute total. Transfer the fish to a plate. Add the garlic cloves to the oil, then remove the wok from the heat and let stand until the garlic turns light golden, about 3 minutes. Using a slotted spoon, transfer the garlic cloves to paper towels to drain.

3. Carefully drain all but 2 teaspoons of the oil from the wok. Heat the remaining oil until smoking. Add the pork and cook over high heat until browned in spots, about 1 minute. Using a slotted spoon, transfer the pork to a plate. Add the garlic cloves and ginger to the wok and stir-fry over moderately high heat until fragrant, about 15 seconds. Return the fish

to the wok and pour in the water. Bring to a boil and add the sherry, sugar and the remaining ¼ cup of soy sauce. Cover and simmer over moderate heat for 3 minutes. Return the pork to the wok and continue to simmer until the fish is white throughout, about 5 minutes. Stir in the cornstarch mixture and cook until the sauce is slightly thickened, about 1 minute.

4. Using 2 spatulas, transfer the fish to a platter. Spoon the sauce over the fish and drizzle with the sesame oil. Sprinkle the fish with the cilantro and scallion and serve.

STEAMED LOBSTER WITH
GARLIC-GINGER-BASIL SAUCE, P. 138

ASIAN FLAVORS OF JEAN-GEORGES

JEAN-GEORGES VONGERICHTEN

PUBLISHED BY BROADWAY BOOKS, $40

Superchef Jean-Georges Vongerichten has 18 restaurants around the world serving the East-West hybrid cuisine he pioneered. This cookbook, his third, re-creates dishes from three of his restaurants: Spice Market, which focuses on Southeast Asian street food, Chinese-inspired 66 (now defunct) and Thai-French Vong. The recipes, which range from a clever (and perfect) Roast Chicken with Chunky Miso Sauce & Grapefruit to a succulent Charred Sirloin with Soy, Garlic & Coriander, are at once surprisingly simple, intensely flavorful and light. Jean-Georges groupies—and anyone else looking for original ideas—will covet this book.

featured recipes Steamed Lobster with Garlic-Ginger-Basil Sauce; Roast Chicken with Chunky Miso Sauce & Grapefruit; Charred Sirloin with Soy, Garlic & Coriander; Chicken Paillard with Napa Salad

best of the best exclusive Steamed Red Snapper & Shiitake with Ginger-Scallion Sauce

Find more recipes by Jean-Georges Vongerichten at foodandwine.com/vongerichten.

STEAMED LOBSTER WITH GARLIC-GINGER-BASIL SAUCE

SERVES 4

Four 1½-pound lobsters, claws separated
½ cup clarified unsalted butter
¼ cup thinly sliced garlic
One 4-inch piece fresh ginger, julienned
1 teaspoon crushed red pepper flakes
1 teaspoon salt, plus more to taste
1 cup chopped fresh Thai basil leaves
8 cups pea shoots and leaves
4 lemon wedges for serving

EDITOR'S NOTE

The pea shoots called for in this recipe are the tender leaves and vines of the pea plant. They have a fresh, sweet, nutty flavor and are sold at Asian markets. The pea sprouts sold at natural-food stores (also often—and confusingly—called pea shoots) will also work here, as will baby spinach.

Here, the classic steamed lobster is completely transformed. This quite elegant dish can be made in less than an hour, even if you must begin by clarifying the butter.

1. Fill a large bowl with water and ice and set aside. Bring a large pot of water to a rolling boil and salt it.

2. Add the lobster claws to the boiling water and cook for 5 minutes, then transfer to the ice water bath. When cool, remove the meat completely from the shells and set aside. Add the remaining lobster parts to the boiling water and cook for 1 minute. Transfer to the ice water bath. When cool, remove the heads from the bodies. Split the tails lengthwise in half, keeping the shells on. (You can remove the vein from the tail if you like.)

3. Prepare the sauce. Put the butter in a large skillet over medium-high heat. Add the garlic and simmer, shaking the skillet occasionally, until golden brown, 3 minutes. Add the ginger, red pepper flakes, and salt and cook, shaking the skillet occasionally, until fragrant. Add the basil and cook briefly, just until wilted. Remove from the heat.

4. Meanwhile, put the claws and tails in a large steamer. Top with the pea shoots and a sprinkling of salt, and cook just until the lobster is heated through and the pea shoots are wilted, about 3 minutes.

5. Mound the pea shoots in the middle of each serving plate and top with the lobster claw meat and tails. Spoon the sauce over the lobster and serve immediately, with the lemon wedges.

ROAST CHICKEN WITH CHUNKY MISO SAUCE & GRAPEFRUIT

SERVES 4

¼ cup plus 1 tablespoon extra-virgin olive oil
One 3-pound chicken, cut into pieces
Salt and freshly ground white pepper
1 cup crème fraîche or sour cream
1 tablespoon chunky miso, or use any miso
1 tablespoon yuzu or lime juice
1 grapefruit, peeled and segmented between membranes, with juices reserved, and chopped into ½-inch cubes
1 fresh red Thai chile, seeded and minced
1 bunch frisée, leaves separated, washed, and dried
1 tablespoon fresh lemon juice

EDITOR'S NOTE
Chunky miso (called *tsubu* miso in Japan) is the more traditional, unblended form, in which whole soybeans are still visible. Smooth, blended miso (*koji* miso) is a newer invention and is more readily available.

This is the quintessential Vong dish, half French and half Asian. But despite the fancy title and complex flavors, it's pretty easy to prepare and is luxuriously creamy when it's done. Substitute romaine or any other crunchy green for the frisée if you like; you can also make this dish with veal, pork, or any white meat.

1. Preheat the oven to 450°F.

2. Heat 2 tablespoons of the oil in a large ovenproof skillet over medium-high heat. Sprinkle the chicken pieces with salt and white pepper and add to the skillet, skin side down. Cook until they are very brown on one side, about 10 minutes, then turn the chicken and transfer to the oven and cook until cooked through, about 10 minutes more.

3. Meanwhile, put the crème fraîche and miso in a saucepan over low heat. Whisk the mixture together and warm gently; do not allow the mixture to boil. When bubbles begin forming around the edges, remove from the heat and whisk in the yuzu juice; set aside.

4. In a bowl, toss the grapefruit and its reserved juices with the chile and 2 tablespoons of the oil. In a separate bowl, toss the frisée with the lemon juice and remaining 1 tablespoon oil and season with salt.

5. Spoon the miso sauce into the bottom of four serving bowls. Center the chicken pieces on the sauce, then spoon the solids from the grapefruit mixture on top. Garnish with the frisée, drizzle on the remaining grapefruit juice, and serve.

CHARRED SIRLOIN WITH SOY, GARLIC & CORIANDER

SERVES 4

- ½ cup light soy sauce
- ¼ cup regular soy sauce
- ½ tablespoon dark soy sauce
- 1 fresh green Thai chile, halved lengthwise
- 1 fresh red Thai chile, halved lengthwise
- 3 dried Thai chiles, seeded and crushed
- 1½ tablespoons coriander seeds, toasted and crushed
- ¼ cup bourbon
- ¼ cup crushed fresh cilantro leaves
- ¼ cup crushed fresh Thai basil leaves
- ¼ cup crushed fresh mint leaves

Four 8-ounce sirloin or ribeye steaks, each about 1 inch thick, at room temperature
- 2 teaspoons garlic salt
- ¼ cup unsalted butter
- 8 cups fresh spinach leaves

Salt
- 1 tablespoon white sesame seeds, toasted

EDITOR'S NOTE

Thai basil has narrow green leaves, purple stems and a pronounced anise flavor. Buy it at Asian markets, or substitute regular basil. If you don't have an array of soy sauces in your pantry, use 1¼ cups of regular soy sauce for this recipe.

As if grilled sirloin weren't good enough already, I infuse it with soy and finish it with a fresh dressing built around coriander. Wilted spinach is the perfect accompaniment. Here's what I do to make garlic salt, and you can do it too: Buy deep-fried garlic (Thai markets sell it) and mix it with salt—the stuff is great!

1. Put the first 8 ingredients into a medium saucepan and set over high heat. Bring to a boil, then immediately remove from the heat and add the cilantro, basil, and mint. Stir well, then set aside to cool, uncovered, to room temperature. When cool, puree in a blender and strain through a fine-mesh sieve, extracting all the liquid; set aside. (You can do this a day or two in advance if you like.)

2. Start a charcoal or gas grill or broiler; the fire should be hot, and the grill rack should be about 5 inches from the heat source.

3. Brush the steaks generously with the soy infusion, reserving any leftover sauce, season with garlic salt, and set on the grill. Cook the first side for 3 minutes, then cook the other side for another 5 minutes for medium-rare. Remove from the grill and let rest.

4. Meanwhile, melt the butter in a large skillet over medium-high heat. When the butter smells nutty, add the spinach and season with salt. Cook, stirring occasionally, just until almost wilted. Then stir in the toasted sesame seeds and divide the spinach evenly among the serving plates.

5. Cut the steaks crosswise into 1-inch slices and brush with the reserved sauce. Put the steak slices on top of the spinach and serve.

CHICKEN PAILLARD WITH NAPA SALAD

SERVES 4

4 cups fresh cilantro leaves

1 teaspoon freshly ground black pepper

One 8-inch block palm sugar, melted, or about ½ cup brown sugar

6 garlic cloves, peeled

½ cup nam pla (Thai fish sauce)

4 boneless, skinless chicken breasts, pounded until less than ½ inch thick

2 fresh red Thai chiles, seeded and finely minced

2 tablespoons granulated sugar

2 teaspoons whole black peppercorns, cracked

1 tablespoon rice vinegar

3 tablespoons fresh lime juice

3 tablespoons grapeseed, corn, or other neutral oil

2 cups thinly sliced Napa cabbage

1 cup shredded carrot

1 cup shredded daikon radish

½ cup sliced red onion

½ cup sliced mango

¼ cup sliced fresh mint leaves, plus more for garnish

Salt

EDITOR'S NOTE

Palm sugar (sometimes sold as coconut sugar) sweetens this refreshingly crunchy, sweet-savory salad. Light brown and usually formed into disks, it is made from the sap of date or coconut palm buds. Look for palm sugar in Asian markets, or use brown sugar.

If you're looking for a refreshing yet substantial summer dish, this is it. Mango and mint add a playful sweetness to this light but assertive salad, which is nicely complemented by the grilled chicken. I love it.

1. Fill a large bowl with water and ice and set aside. Bring a small pot of water to a boil and add the cilantro. As soon as the water returns to a boil, drain the leaves, and transfer to the ice water. When cold, drain again, and transfer to a blender with the ground pepper, palm sugar, 4 garlic cloves, and half the nam pla. Puree until smooth. Spread a thin coat of this paste on the chicken breasts and marinate in the refrigerator for about 1 hour.

2. Meanwhile, make the salad. Mince the remaining garlic cloves, transfer to a mixing bowl, and whisk with the chiles, granulated sugar, peppercorns, vinegar, lime juice, oil, and remaining ¼ cup nam pla. In a large bowl, toss half the dressing with the cabbage, carrot, radish, onion, mango, and mint.

3. Start a charcoal or gas grill or broiler; the fire should be medium-hot and the grill rack should be about 4 inches from the heat source.

4. Grill the chicken breasts with the marinade until they are cooked through, 3 to 4 minutes a side. Cut the cooked breasts into 1-inch slices.

5. Mound the salad on a plate and top with another spoonful of dressing and the slices of chicken. Garnish with mint leaves, sprinkle lightly with salt, and serve.

best of the best exclusive

STEAMED RED SNAPPER & SHIITAKE WITH GINGER-SCALLION SAUCE

SERVES 4

- ½ cup minced fresh ginger
- 2 scallions, thinly sliced
- 1 stalk of fresh lemongrass, tender inner white bulb only, minced
- 1 small jalapeño, seeded and minced
- ½ cup grapeseed oil
- ¼ cup white miso paste
- 1 tablespoon Asian sesame oil
- 1 tablespoon Asian fish sauce
- 2 tablespoons finely chopped tarragon
- 2 tablespoons finely chopped cilantro
- 1 tablespoon finely grated orange zest
- 4 snapper fillets (about 6 ounces each)
- 10 ounces shiitake mushrooms, stems discarded, caps quartered

Kosher salt and freshly ground pepper
Extra-virgin olive oil, for drizzling

EDITOR'S NOTE

Vongerichten calls for the herb *rau ram* for this elegant dish. Also known as Vietnamese coriander, it has pointy green leaves and a spicy, minty flavor. We replaced the *rau ram* with cilantro, but if you find *rau ram* at an Asian market, use it for a more authentic flavor.

1. In a heatproof medium bowl, mix the ginger with the scallions, lemongrass and jalapeño. In a small skillet, heat the grapeseed oil over moderately high heat until wisps of smoke appear. Pour the hot oil over the ginger mixture. Stir in the miso paste, sesame oil, fish sauce, tarragon, cilantro and orange zest.

2. Set a bamboo steamer over a wok full of water and bring to a boil. Place the snapper and mushrooms in the steamer, season with salt and pepper and drizzle lightly with olive oil. Cover and steam over moderately high heat until the snapper is cooked through and the mushrooms are tender, about 12 minutes. Transfer the snapper and mushrooms to plates. Spoon some of the ginger-scallion sauce on top and serve.

PICKLED CHINESE CABBAGE
WITH CHILE, P. 146

MY CHINA

KYLIE KWONG

PUBLISHED BY VIKING STUDIO, $55

Australian star chef Kylie Kwong comes from the oldest and largest Chinese family in Australia—her great-grandfather was one of the earliest Chinese immigrants—but she often asks herself, "Am I really Australian, or am I more Chinese?" In *My China,* Kwong sets out on a journey to Asia, not only to learn about her ancestors but also to delve into Chinese food and culture. This book is a compelling travelogue, with lots of practical tips (when ordering at a restaurant, pointing at food on other people's plates is acceptable); even better, it offers excellent, easy Chinese recipes, like silky, sweet-spicy Kung Po Chicken, thanks to Kwong's rare ability to approach authentic Chinese recipes with a Western sensibility.

featured recipes Pickled Chinese Cabbage with Chile; Stir-Fried Rice Noodles with Black Beans, Chiles & Coriander; Kung Po Chicken; Steamed Chicken with Hot & Sour Dressing

best of the best exclusive Chile-Salt Duck Breasts with Lemon & Mint

PICKLED CHINESE CABBAGE
WITH CHILE

SERVES 4 TO 6
AS PART OF A SHARED MEAL

- 1 medium Chinese cabbage—about 750 grams (1 pound 8 ounces)—cut into 2.5-centimeter (1-inch) squares
- 3 tablespoons sea salt
- 2 tablespoons brown sugar
- ⅓ cup peanut oil
- 1 tablespoon Sichuan peppercorns
- 6 small dried red chiles
- 2 tablespoons brown rice vinegar
- 1 large red chile, finely sliced

EDITOR'S NOTE

Chinese cabbage is often sold as napa cabbage. Brown rice vinegar is sold at health-food stores, but regular unseasoned rice vinegar is a fine substitute.

Combine cabbage in a bowl with salt and sugar, mix well and leave to stand for 2 hours.

Place oil, Sichuan peppercorns and dried chiles in a cold wok and *then* turn heat to high. Cook for about 30 seconds or until peppercorns and chiles begin to darken. Remove wok from stove and carefully strain flavored oil through a metal sieve into a large bowl. Discard peppercorns and chiles, and set oil aside to cool.

Drain cabbage and, using your hands, gently squeeze out any excess liquid. Place cabbage in bowl containing flavored oil, then add vinegar and fresh chile and mix well.

STIR-FRIED RICE NOODLES WITH BLACK BEANS, CHILES & CORIANDER

SERVES 4 TO 6
AS PART OF A SHARED MEAL

500 grams (1 pound) fresh rice
     noodle sheets
  ¼ cup peanut oil
  2 tablespoons salted black beans
  ⅓ cup finely chopped coriander
     (cilantro) roots and stems
  2 large red chiles, finely chopped
  2 tablespoons light soy sauce
  1 tablespoon dark soy sauce
  1 teaspoon sesame oil

EDITOR'S NOTE
Fresh rice noodles have a lovely chewiness that makes this dish delicious. Look for them (either in sheets or cut into noodles) at Asian markets; it's best to use them the same day you buy them, as they tend to clump together in the fridge. If fresh noodles are not available, the dish is still wonderful with dried.

Cut noodle sheets into 1-centimeter (½-inch) strips and carefully separate them.

Heat peanut oil in a hot wok until surface seems to shimmer slightly. Add black beans, coriander and chile and stir-fry for 1½ minutes, stirring constantly to ensure the black beans do not burn. Toss in rice noodles and stir-fry for 1 minute.

Add remaining ingredients and stir-fry for a further 3 minutes or until noodles are heated through. Serve immediately.

KUNG PO CHICKEN

SERVES 4 TO 6
AS PART OF A SHARED MEAL

600 grams (1 pound 4 ounces) chicken
    thigh fillets, cut into 1-centimeter
    (½-inch) cubes
  2 tablespoons cornflour (cornstarch)
  2 tablespoons shao hsing wine
  2 tablespoons peanut oil
 10 small dried red chiles
  2 tablespoons peanut oil, extra
5-centimeter (2-inch) piece ginger,
    cut into thin strips
  1 tablespoon brown sugar
  ½ cup roasted unsalted peanuts
  2 tablespoons light soy sauce
  1 tablespoon Chinese black vinegar
Pinch Sichuan pepper and salt

EDITOR'S NOTE
Marinating ingredients in
cornstarch and wine is a Chinese
technique known as silkening. It
gives food a tender, velvety texture.

Although I have eaten several versions of Kung Po chicken in Chinese restaurants around the world, none of them prepared me for this lip-smacking authentic version. A mouth-watering combination of fried chicken cubes, chiles and peanuts dressed with soy sauce and black vinegar, Kung Po chicken (or gongbao jiding in Chinese, meaning "Governor's Diced Chicken") is named after a nineteenth-century Sichuanese governor.

Combine chicken with cornflour and shao hsing wine in a bowl. Cover, place in refrigerator and leave to marinate for 1 hour.

Place oil and chiles in a cold wok and *then* turn heat to low. Cook for about 1½ minutes or until chiles begin to darken slightly. Using a slotted spoon, immediately remove chiles and drain on kitchen paper.

Leaving chile-infused oil in wok, turn heat up to high and stir-fry half the chicken cubes for 3 minutes. Remove with a slotted spoon. Add extra oil to wok with remaining chicken and stir-fry for 3 minutes. Return all chicken to wok, along with ginger and reserved chiles and stir-fry for 30 seconds.

Add sugar and stir-fry for 30 seconds. Add peanuts, soy sauce and vinegar and stir-fry for 30 seconds. Serve immediately, sprinkled with Sichuan pepper and salt.

STEAMED CHICKEN WITH HOT & SOUR DRESSING

SERVES 4 TO 6
AS PART OF A SHARED MEAL

400 grams (13 ounces) chicken
    thigh fillets

DRESSING
  2 tablespoons finely chopped
     coriander (cilantro) stems
5-centimeter (2-inch) piece ginger,
     cut into thin strips
  2 tablespoons trimmed and finely
     sliced spring onions (scallions)
  2 garlic cloves, finely chopped
  1 large red chile, finely sliced
2½ tablespoons light soy sauce
  1 tablespoon brown rice vinegar
  1 teaspoon brown sugar
  1 teaspoon sesame oil
  2 tablespoons peanut oil

First, make the dressing. Combine all ingredients except peanut oil in a heatproof bowl. Heat peanut oil in a small heavy-based pan until surface shimmers slightly, then carefully pour over ingredients in bowl. Stir to combine and set aside, uncovered.

Arrange chicken in a single layer on a heatproof plate that will fit inside a steamer basket. Place plate inside steamer, position over a deep saucepan or wok of boiling water and steam, covered, for about 14 minutes or until chicken is just tender. Remove plate from steamer basket and allow chicken to rest for 5 minutes.

Drain off excess liquid and transfer chicken to a chopping board. Cut chicken on the diagonal into 1-centimeter (½-inch) slices and arrange on a platter. Spoon over dressing and serve at room temperature.

best of the best exclusive

CHILE-SALT DUCK BREASTS WITH LEMON & MINT

SERVES 6

1½ teaspoons Sichuan peppercorns
2½ tablespoons kosher salt
4 moulard duck breasts (3 pounds)
2 tablespoons all-purpose flour
1 tablespoon pure mild chile powder, such as New Mexico
Vegetable oil, for frying
2 scallions, thinly sliced lengthwise and cut into 2-inch lengths
¼ cup mint leaves, thinly sliced
1 long red chile, such as Holland, thinly sliced on the diagonal
2 lemons, halved

1. In a small skillet, toast the Sichuan peppercorns with 1½ tablespoons of the salt over moderate heat until fragrant, about 3 minutes. Transfer to a spice grinder and process to a fine powder. Transfer the Sichuan pepper–salt to a small bowl.

2. In a large saucepan fitted with a steamer basket, bring 1 inch of water to a boil. Arrange the duck breasts skin side up in the steamer basket, cover and steam over moderate heat for 10 minutes. Transfer the duck to a plate and let stand until cool enough to handle, about 10 minutes.

3. Pat the duck breasts dry. In a pie plate, mix the remaining 1 tablespoon of salt with the flour and chile powder. Dust the duck with the flour mixture and shake off any excess.

4. In a large, deep skillet, heat ½ inch of oil until shimmering. Add the duck breasts skin side down and cook over moderately high heat until the skin begins to crisp, about 3 minutes. Turn the duck breasts over and cook until pink in the center, about 2 minutes. Transfer the duck to a cutting board and let rest for 5 minutes.

EDITOR'S NOTE
Sichuan peppercorns are dried rust-colored berries that can slightly numb the tongue. Until recently they could not be imported into the U.S., but now they're available at Asian markets and from penzeys.com. You can also forgo the Sichuan pepper–salt here; the duck has plenty of flavor without it.

5. Slice the duck on the diagonal ¼ inch thick and transfer to plates. Top each breast with some of the scallions, mint and chile slices. Serve with lemon and the Sichuan pepper–salt, for sprinkling.

SERVE WITH Steamed white rice.

MAKE AHEAD The Sichuan pepper–salt can be made up to 1 month ahead.

THE SEVENTH DAUGHTER

CECILIA CHIANG WITH LISA WEISS

PUBLISHED BY TEN SPEED PRESS, $35

"One misconception about me is that I have grown up in the kitchen. The truth is, for most of my early life, I was really just a good eater," writes 88-year-old Cecilia Chiang. As children growing up in a wealthy family in Beijing, Chiang and her sisters weren't even allowed in the kitchen, but Chiang still managed to absorb a lot from watching the family cooks and her mother. Then, when she turned 40 and moved to San Francisco, she found herself—somewhat impulsively—opening a Chinese restaurant, The Mandarin. In *The Seventh Daughter,* Chiang tells her compelling life story and shares dozens of the recipes that made The Mandarin such a success, including a succulent stir-fry of beef and snow peas, along with favorite dishes from her childhood, like the unusual and irresistible star anise–spiced peanuts her father loved.

featured recipes Stir-Fried Beef with Snow Peas; Prawns "à la Szechwan"; Star-Anise Peanuts; Steamed Black Bass with Ginger & Green Onions

best of the best exclusive Crispy Chinese Chicken

STIR-FRIED BEEF WITH SNOW PEAS
HE LAN DOU CHAO NIU ROU

**SERVES 6 TO 8 AS PART OF A
CHINESE MEAL AND 4 TO 6 AS
A WESTERN-STYLE ENTRÉE**

- 1 pound flank steak
- 3½ tablespoons peanut oil
- 1 teaspoon baking soda
- 2 teaspoons cornstarch
- ½ teaspoon freshly ground
  white pepper
- Pinch of kosher salt
- 1 tablespoon oyster sauce
- ¾ pound (about 4 cups) fresh
  snow peas, ends snapped
  and strings removed
- Freshly ground black pepper,
  for finishing

For a long time I didn't get it. What was the deal with snow peas? In the early days of The Mandarin, it seemed everyone thought they were some exotic Chinese vegetable. I'd never even tasted a snow pea until I ate them at a Cantonese restaurant with my future husband when I lived in Sichuan Province during the war. Snow peas are not grown in northern China, only in the southern part of the country, and in fact it's the Cantonese word shui dou *that translates to "snow pea" in English.*

So the flank steak is easier to slice, freeze it for 30 minutes or so to firm it up. Halve the frozen beef lengthwise, then with your knife almost parallel to the cutting surface, slice it diagonally against the grain into thin slices, about ⅛ inch thick.

TO MARINATE THE BEEF Toss the slices with 1½ tablespoons of the peanut oil, baking soda, cornstarch, and white pepper in a medium bowl. Cover the bowl and let the beef marinate in the refrigerator for 1 hour.

Heat a large wok over high heat until a bead of water dances on the surface and then evaporates. Add the remaining 2 tablespoons of oil with a pinch of salt and swirl to coat the pan. Toss in the beef and cook, stirring constantly, 2 to 3 minutes, or until the beef has started to brown. Add the oyster sauce and stir to combine well. Continue to cook 30 seconds more, or until the pieces are still a bit pink. Transfer the beef to a bowl. Set aside.

Return the pan to high heat, add the snow peas, and cook 30 seconds, tossing constantly. Stir in the reserved beef and continue to cook 30 seconds more. Transfer the beef to a serving platter and sprinkle with freshly ground black pepper.

NOTES

To make this dish special, you need extremely fresh snow peas. Look for ones that are smooth, unwrinkled, and slightly translucent, with only teeny-tiny pea bumps in their pods. Don't buy any that have already been stringed and cut on the ends; the processing that's required to do this makes them too old. You can tell if they're fresh if the ends crisply snap off when you bend them.

The freshly ground black pepper added just before serving wasn't something Cecilia would normally add, but was just what this simple dish needed to give it a little oomph.

—*Lisa Weiss*

PRAWNS "À LA SZECHWAN"
GAN SHAO MING XIA

**SERVES 6 TO 8 AS PART OF A
CHINESE MEAL AND 4 TO 6 AS
A WESTERN-STYLE ENTRÉE**

- 1 pound medium shrimp, shelled, tails removed, and deveined
- 2 teaspoons kosher salt, plus a pinch for the wok
- 2 teaspoons cornstarch
- 3 tablespoons plus 2 teaspoons peanut oil
- 2 tablespoons Shaoxing wine
- 2 tablespoons soy sauce
- 2 tablespoons sugar
- ¼ cup ketchup
- 2 teaspoons Asian sesame oil
- 2 teaspoons minced garlic
- 2 teaspoons minced fresh ginger
- 2 teaspoons red pepper flakes

Thinly sliced green onions, for garnish

If I were to give a more accurate English name to this dish it would be Sichuan Shrimp. I guess I thought Prawns à la Szechwan sounded fancier when I wrote the first menus at The Mandarin. But that was at a time when the only fine-dining restaurants were primarily French. The name for the dish stuck, and when we moved to Ghirardelli Square, Prawns à la Szechwan remained one of our best sellers.

In a bowl, gently mix the shrimp with 2 teaspoons of the salt to coat well. Cover the shrimp with cold water and slosh them around a few times. Drain well and transfer the shrimp to a clean bowl. Mix the shrimp with the cornstarch and 2 teaspoons of the peanut oil. Set aside for 5 minutes.

TO MAKE THE SAUCE Whisk together the wine, soy sauce, sugar, ketchup, and sesame oil in a small bowl until well combined. Set aside.

TO COOK THE SHRIMP Heat a large wok over high heat until a bead of water dances on the surface and then evaporates. Add the remaining 3 tablespoons of peanut oil and a pinch of salt and swirl to coat the pan. Add the garlic, ginger, and pepper flakes, stirring constantly for 10 seconds. Toss in the shrimp and stir-fry until they are just pink, about 1 minute. Pour in the reserved sauce, bring the liquid to a boil, and toss to coat the shrimp well. Immediately remove the pan from the heat, as you don't want to overcook the shrimp.

To serve, turn the shrimp out onto a platter, sprinkle with a few green onion slices, and serve hot.

NOTE My husband, Dan, who loves spicy food, but isn't too crazy about shrimp, thought this was one of the best dishes we tested. His only suggestion was that it could be spicier, so add more red pepper flakes if you're so inclined. Consider serving the shrimp as an hors d'oeuvre, skewered on toothpicks. —*Lisa Weiss*

STAR-ANISE PEANUTS
WU XIANG HUA SHENG MI

MAKES ABOUT 3 CUPS

- 12 ounces skinless shelled raw peanuts (see Notes on p. 162)
- 6 whole star anise (see Notes on p. 162)
- 2 tablespoons kosher salt
- 1 tablespoon soy sauce
- 2 teaspoons sugar

EDITOR'S NOTE
These boiled peanuts are nothing like regular peanuts. They are crisp, like water chestnuts, with a lovely, salty, Asian flavor from the soy sauce and star anise.

Hua sheng *means "flowering peanuts," probably so named because of the blossom shape of the star anise. They were a favorite of my father's and made frequent appearances as part of his nightly* jiu cai, *or "little wine dishes." They're a little salty, a little sweet, a little crunchy, and very addictive. Allison Saunders, who tested many of the recipes for this book, ate so many of them during the test, we probably should offer a disclaimer on the yield.*

In a saucepan, add the peanuts and enough water to cover them generously. Bring to a boil over high heat, decrease the heat to medium-low and simmer, skimming off the foam with a slotted spoon.

After about 5 minutes (or when the foaming stops), stir in the star anise, salt, and soy sauce. Cook 30 minutes more, adding more water as needed to keep the peanuts moving freely in the liquid. Stir in the sugar, and cook 5 minutes more, or until the peanuts are soft, but still have a little resistance when you bite them.

continued on p. 162

Remove the pan from the heat and let the peanuts cool in the liquid. Drain, transfer to a covered container, and refrigerate for up to 5 days.

The peanuts can be served chilled or at room temperature.

NOTES

Both Asian markets and natural food stores often carry shelled raw peanuts, both skin-on and skinless. You can skin peanuts yourself, if you need to. When you put the shelled peanuts in the saucepan with the water as you proceed with this recipe, skim off the loose skins that float to the top. Do this two or three times, continuing to remove any loose skins as they cook.

If you'd like a stronger star anise flavor, feel free to add a few more to the cooking liquid. —*Lisa Weiss*

STEAMED BLACK BASS WITH GINGER & GREEN ONIONS
QING ZHENG HEI BAN YU

**SERVES 4 TO 6 AS PART OF A
CHINESE MEAL OR 2 TO 4 AS
A WESTERN-STYLE ENTRÉE**

- 1 small, very fresh whole black bass, striped bass, rock cod, or snapper (about 1 to 1½ pounds), cleaned and scaled, with head and tail left on (see Note on p. 164)
- 6 large paper-thin slices peeled fresh ginger
- 2 tablespoons Shaoxing wine
- 2 tablespoons peanut oil
- 3 tablespoons premium soy sauce
- 1 tablespoon oyster sauce
- 2-inch piece fresh ginger, peeled and cut in julienne pieces, for garnish
- 2 green onions, white parts only, thinly sliced lengthwise and cut crosswise into 2-inch strips
- ¼ cup fresh cilantro leaves, for garnish

At the conclusion of every New Year's Eve banquet we always looked forward to the arrival of the fish. No matter how it was prepared—steamed or fried—it was served whole, with its head and tail intact, representing a good beginning and good ending to the year. (My uncles and father used to fight over the fish cheeks and tails.) This preparation is typically Cantonese (who have mastered the art of steam-cooked foods) and I love it for its ease and simplicity. I often will steam a small whole fish just for myself at home and to make cooking even easier, I use the microwave.

TO PREPARE THE FISH With a sharp knife held at an angle, make 3 slashes about 1 to 1½ inches apart in the flesh of both sides of the fish, almost to the bone. Stuff each slash with 1 slice of ginger. Place the fish on a rimmed plate that fits inside a steamer. (If the fish is too long, you can curl it up.) Drizzle 1 tablespoon of the wine over the fish.

Fill a steamer bottom with about 2 inches of water and bring to a boil over high heat. Place the plate with the fish in a steamer tier and set over the boiling water. Cover and steam 5 minutes.

continued on p. 164

EDITOR'S NOTE
To make sure the fish is cooked through, use a knife to peek into one of the slits to see if the flesh is opaque and separates easily from the bone.

While the fish is steaming, bring the peanut oil to a boil in a small saucepan over medium heat. Keep the oil hot until ready to use.

TO MAKE THE SAUCE Whisk together the remaining tablespoon of wine, soy sauce, and oyster sauce in a small bowl. Set aside.

When the fish is cooked, carefully lift the plate out of the steamer tier and transfer the fish to a platter. Garnish with the ginger, green onions, and cilantro. Drizzle the sauce over the top of and around the fish. Pour over the hot oil and serve.

NOTE We recommend using small whole fish, about 1½ pounds, because unless you have a large steamer (or a fish poacher), any fish larger than that is difficult to work with. If you want to microwave the fish, as Cecilia sometimes likes to do, put it in a covered baking dish for 3 minutes.
—*Lisa Weiss*

best of the best exclusive

CRISPY CHINESE CHICKEN

SERVES 4

- 2 chicken breast halves on the bone, with skin (1½ pounds), halved crosswise
- 2 whole chicken legs (1 pound), legs and thighs separated
- 1 tablespoon kosher salt
- 2 tablespoons Shaoxing wine
- 3 scallions, 2 cut into 2-inch pieces and 1 thinly sliced
- 2 star anise pods, broken into pieces

Two ¼-inch-thick slices of fresh ginger
Vegetable oil, for frying
- ½ teaspoon ground Sichuan peppercorns (see Note)

EDITOR'S NOTE

For a head start on this recipe, you can marinate and steam the chicken a day in advance, then refrigerate it. Let it return to room temperature before frying.

1. Set the chicken on a work surface and rub it all over with 2½ teaspoons of the salt. In a large bowl, toss the chicken with the wine, scallion pieces, star anise and ginger. Refrigerate for 3 hours, turning the chicken once halfway.

2. Transfer the chicken and all of the marinade ingredients to a large plate. Set the plate in a bamboo steamer set over a wok of boiling water. Cover and steam the chicken over moderately high heat for about 25 minutes, until cooked through. Discard the scallions, star anise and ginger. Dry the chicken well with paper towels.

3. In a large saucepan, heat 3 inches of oil to 350°F. Fry the chicken in batches until golden and crisp, about 4 minutes. Drain on paper towels.

4. In a small bowl, mix the remaining ½ teaspoon of salt with the ground Sichuan peppercorns. Transfer the chicken to a platter and sprinkle it with the sliced scallion and some of the Sichuan pepper–salt. Serve at once.

NOTE Sichuan peppercorns are available at Asian markets or online from penzeys.com.

MAKING DINNER FOR FRIENDS

ANTIPASTO SALAD, P. 170

EVERYDAY PASTA

GIADA DE LAURENTIIS

PUBLISHED BY CLARKSON POTTER, $32.50

"Pasta provides a perfect neutral canvas on which to combine flavors and ingredients," writes Food Network star Giada De Laurentiis in this eminently practical cookbook. Clearly dedicated to fast cooking, De Laurentiis also has a good time creating variations on basic soups, pasta salads, baked pastas (like lasagna) and more. She tops wagon wheel pasta with artichoke pesto instead of the usual basil pesto, and tosses orzo in a creamy tomato sauce with peas (a dish kids will love). The book is exceptionally easy to cook from, with lots of photos and very straightforward instructions.

featured recipes Antipasto Salad; Creamy Orzo; Wagon Wheels with Artichoke Pesto

Find more recipes by Giada De Laurentiis at foodandwine.com/delaurentiis.

ANTIPASTO SALAD

SERVES 4 TO 6

VINAIGRETTE

  1   bunch of fresh basil, stemmed
       and chopped (about 2 cups)
  ¼   cup red wine vinegar
  1   garlic clove, halved
  1   teaspoon Dijon mustard
  ½   teaspoon salt
  ½   teaspoon freshly ground
       black pepper
  ¾   cup extra-virgin olive oil

ANTIPASTO SALAD

  1   pound fusilli pasta
  ½   cup hard salami cut into strips
       (about 3 ounces)
  ½   cup smoked turkey cut into strips
       (about 3 ounces)
  ¼   cup Provolone cheese cut into strips
  ¼   cup grated Asiago cheese
  2   tablespoons pitted and halved
       green olives
  2   tablespoons roasted red peppers
       cut into strips
  ¼   teaspoon salt
  ½   teaspoon freshly ground
       black pepper

When we're hosting game night and have lots of my husband's friends coming over, I make this salad. It's hearty and colorful, and because it holds very well at room temperature, I can make it ahead of time so I can take part in game night, too!

In a blender, combine the basil, vinegar, garlic, mustard, salt, and pepper. Blend until the basil and garlic are finely chopped. With the machine running, drizzle in the olive oil until the dressing is smooth.

Bring a large pot of salted water to a boil over high heat. Add the pasta and cook until it's tender, stirring occasionally, 10 to 12 minutes. Drain.

In a large bowl, toss together the cooked pasta with the remaining salad ingredients. Drizzle with the dressing and toss to coat.

CREAMY ORZO

SERVES 6 TO 8

  1 pound orzo (rice-shaped pasta)
  2 tablespoons olive oil
  1 large shallot, finely chopped
  1 garlic clove, minced
  1 (14.5-ounce) can diced tomatoes, drained
1¼ cups heavy cream
  1 cup frozen peas, thawed
  ¾ cup freshly grated Parmesan cheese
Salt and freshly ground black pepper

EDITOR'S NOTE
Feel free to use any frozen vegetables here in place of the peas. Chopped ham or prosciutto would be delicious in this creamy dish, too.

Kids go crazy for this dish. It's creamy, colorful, and, best of all, they can eat it with a spoon!

Bring a large, heavy saucepan of salted water to a boil over high heat. Add the orzo and cook until tender but still firm to the bite, stirring often, about 8 minutes. Drain, reserving 1 cup of the pasta water.

Meanwhile, heat the oil in a large, heavy frying pan over medium heat. Add the shallot and garlic, and sauté until tender, about 2 minutes. Add the tomatoes and cook until they are tender, about 8 minutes. Stir in the cream and peas. Add the orzo and toss to coat. Remove the skillet from the heat. Add the Parmesan cheese to the pasta mixture and toss to coat. Stir the pasta mixture until the sauce coats the pasta thickly, adding enough of the reserved pasta water to create a creamy consistency. Season with salt and pepper and serve.

WAGON WHEELS
WITH ARTICHOKE PESTO

SERVES 4 TO 6

- 1 pound rotelle (wagon wheel pasta)
- 1 (8-ounce) package of frozen artichoke hearts, thawed
- 1 cup fresh flat-leaf parsley leaves, lightly packed
- ½ cup chopped toasted walnuts
- Zest and juice of 1 lemon
- 1 garlic clove
- ½ teaspoon kosher salt
- ½ teaspoon freshly ground black pepper
- ¾ cup extra-virgin olive oil
- ⅔ cup freshly grated Parmesan cheese

EDITOR'S NOTE

This nutty, fresh-tasting pesto is wonderful spread on sandwiches, or served with pita chips as a Mediterranean-style dip.

Who says pesto has to contain basil—or pine nuts, for that matter? This pesto is luxurious and a pretty, pale green; it makes an unbelievably sophisticated meal in just a matter of minutes. I would also serve this as an elegant first course for a spring meal of lamb or salmon.

Bring a large pot of salted water to a boil over high heat. Add the pasta and cook until tender but still firm to the bite, stirring occasionally, 8 to 10 minutes. Drain the pasta, reserving ½ cup of the pasta cooking water.

Meanwhile, in a food processor combine the artichokes, parsley, walnuts, lemon zest and juice, garlic, salt, and pepper. Chop the ingredients fine, stopping the machine a few times to scrape down the sides. With the motor running, drizzle in the olive oil. Transfer the artichoke pesto to a large serving bowl and stir in the cheese. Add the warm pasta and toss to combine. If needed, add the reserved pasta water ¼ cup at a time to moisten the pasta and create a saucelike consistency. Serve.

Evan Lobel at the butcher block.

LOBEL'S PRIME TIME GRILLING

STANLEY, LEON, EVAN, MARK & DAVID LOBEL

PUBLISHED BY JOHN WILEY & SONS, INC., $27.95

"One thing never changes. We understand and revere good butchering."
So say the Lobels, the family of butchers who opened Lobel's Prime Meats in Manhattan in 1954. In this, their fourth cookbook, the Lobels apply their vast knowledge of meat and poultry to grilling. At the beginning of each chapter, they explain in detail how to select and handle a different kind of meat or poultry, then offer their best advice for grilling or smoking it. As in all of their books, the recipes are top-notch, like the bacon-mushroom burger, for which they recommend a combination of ground chuck and sirloin; the sirloin gives the burger a great beefy flavor, while the chuck makes it supremely juicy.

featured recipes Mint-Brushed Lamb Chops; Buttermilk-Soaked Chicken Legs & Thighs; Bacon-Mushroom Burger; Grilled Moroccan-Style Rock Cornish Game Hens

best of the best exclusive Beef Jerky

Find more recipes by the Lobels at foodandwine.com/lobel.

MINT-BRUSHED LAMB CHOPS

SERVES 6

½ cup cider vinegar
2 teaspoons sugar
½ cup coarsely chopped
fresh mint
12 loin lamb chops, each about
2 inches thick
Vegetable oil cooking spray
Freshly ground black pepper to taste

EDITOR'S NOTE

Basting the chops with a minty, vinegar-based marinade gives them a great tangy-fresh flavor. We found that seasoning the lamb with a pinch of kosher salt just before grilling added more depth.

Lamb chops are small, juicy, utterly irresistible treasures. Loin chops are deliciously tender, with a small T-bone that separates the tenderloin from the eye. Rib chops match loin chops in flavor and tenderness. These are the chops from a rack of lamb, and while they have no tenderloin, they are tasty. If you choose to grill them, watch them carefully, as they may take a little less time to cook.

1. Combine the vinegar and sugar in a small bowl and stir until the sugar dissolves. Transfer to a blender and add the mint. Blend until the mint is finely chopped. Brush on both sides of the chops and set aside at room temperature for about 10 minutes. Reserve some of the mixture to brush on the chops during grilling.

2. Prepare a charcoal or gas grill: Lightly spray the grill rack with vegetable oil cooking spray. Light the coals or heating elements, and let them burn or heat until moderately hot to hot.

3. Grill the chops for 6 to 8 minutes on each side until medium-rare, or they are cooked to the desired degree of doneness. Baste with the vinegar mixture several times during grilling. Watch for flare-ups. If they occur, move the chops to a cooler part of the grill and extinguish the flames with a spritz of water. Then move the chops back to the hot fire. Season with pepper just before serving.

BUTTERMILK-SOAKED CHICKEN LEGS & THIGHS

SERVES 6 TO 8

- 4 whole chicken legs, legs and thighs separated (4½ to 5 pounds)
- 3 cups buttermilk
- 2 large shallots, thinly sliced
- 3 large cloves garlic, crushed
- 3 tablespoons roughly chopped fresh thyme
- 2 teaspoons cayenne
- 2 teaspoons celery seed
- 1 teaspoon salt
- ½ teaspoon freshly ground black pepper
- Vegetable oil cooking spray

EDITOR'S NOTE

This marinade works beautifully for chicken breasts as well—the buttermilk keeps them moist.

We have long believed that some of our customers overlook the best-tasting part of the chicken: the legs and thighs. These constitute the dark meat portions of the bird—by definition the more flavorful parts. Plus, these are more economical than the breasts. What do you have to lose? Buy the whole leg, with the thigh attached, and cut them in half. Wiggle the leg at the joint so that you know where to cut. Believe us: this is very easy. Here, we soak these parts in a mildly seasoned buttermilk marinade for chicken with good, old-fashioned flavor.

1. Rinse and pat dry the chicken legs and thighs. Divide them between two large resealable plastic bags or shallow glass or ceramic dishes.

2. Whisk together the remaining ingredients. Divide the marinade between the bags or dishes. Seal the bags or cover the dishes with plastic wrap and refrigerate for at least 2 hours and up to 4 hours, letting the chicken come to room temperature before grilling.

3. Prepare a charcoal or gas grill: Lightly spray the grill rack with vegetable oil cooking spray. Light the coals or heating elements, and let them burn or heat until moderately hot.

4. Lift the chicken from the dish, allowing the excess marinade to drip off. Discard the marinade.

5. Grill the chicken legs and thighs for 40 to 45 minutes, turning often with tongs. The chicken is done when the juices run clear when pierced with a fork or sharp knife, or when an instant-read thermometer registers 180°F inserted in the thickest part of the thighs. Don't let the thermometer touch the bone. Serve immediately.

BACON-MUSHROOM BURGER

SERVES 6

6 slices bacon (about 3 ounces total)
1 pound ground beef sirloin
1 pound ground beef chuck
¼ cup plus 2 tablespoons chopped onion
¼ cup plus 2 tablespoons chopped white mushrooms
Salt and freshly ground black pepper to taste
Vegetable oil cooking spray

EDITOR'S NOTE
We tried these juicy burgers with fresh shiitake in place of the white mushrooms and loved the intense, woodsy flavor they added.

For this burger, which has become what we call a "pub favorite" in America, we combine ground chuck with ground sirloin. If you prefer, you can use one or the other, but remember that a burger made with chuck alone will be juicy but lack the deep flavor of sirloin, while a burger made with sirloin alone will be a little drier. However, the bacon, although cooked, and the mushrooms add a little moisture.

1. Cook the bacon over medium heat in a skillet until cooked but not crispy. Drain on paper towels and when cool enough to handle, tear or chop into small pieces.

2. Combine the beef, bacon, onion, mushrooms, and salt and pepper in a large bowl. Using your hands, mix well. Form into 6 patties. Refrigerate until ready to grill.

3. Prepare a charcoal or gas grill: Lightly spray the grill rack with vegetable oil cooking spray. Light the coals or heating elements, and let them burn or heat until hot.

4. Grill the burgers for about 5 minutes. Turn and grill for 4 or 5 minutes longer for medium-well burgers.

GRILLED MOROCCAN-STYLE ROCK CORNISH GAME HENS

SERVES 4

½ cup peanut oil
¼ cup fresh lemon juice
2 tablespoons chopped fresh cilantro
2 tablespoons chopped flat-leaf parsley
2 cloves garlic, minced
1 tablespoon sweet paprika
2 teaspoons ground cinnamon
2 teaspoons ground turmeric
2 teaspoons ground allspice
2 teaspoons minced fresh ginger
2 teaspoons minced lemon zest
Four 1- to 1¼-pound Rock Cornish game hens
Vegetable oil cooking spray

EDITOR'S NOTE
These marinated hens are great cooked in the oven, too: Place them in a baking dish and roast at 425°F until the juices run clear at the thickest part of the meat, about 45 minutes. Whether you choose to grill or roast these hens, we suggest sprinkling a little salt on them just before cooking.

Rock Cornish game hens are tiny birds that have caught on with Americans, often connoting elegant dining. The miniature birds were the brainchild of poultry breeder Jacques Makowsky, who crossed Cornish game cocks with Plymouth Rock hens at his Connecticut farm. Since their debut in 1950, the tender hens have rapidly grown in popularity.

1. Combine the oil, lemon juice, cilantro, parsley, garlic, paprika, cinnamon, turmeric, allspice, ginger, and lemon zest in a small bowl and stir until well mixed.

2. Put the hens in a shallow glass or ceramic dish and pour the marinade over them. Rub it over the hens and inside the cavities. Using kitchen twine, truss the hens. Cover and refrigerate for at least 6 hours or overnight, letting the hens come to room temperature before grilling.

3. Prepare a charcoal or gas grill: Lightly spray the grill rack with vegetable oil cooking spray. Light the coals or heating elements, and let them burn or heat until moderately hot.

4. Lift the hens from the dish. Discard the marinade. Grill, breast side down, for about 15 minutes. Turn and grill for 25 to 30 minutes longer, until the juices run clear when the thickest part of the meat is pricked with a fork or sharp knife, or when an instant-read thermometer inserted in the thickest meat registers 180°F. Let rest for about 5 minutes before serving.

Clearing.

LOBEL'S PRIME TIME GRILLING

STANLEY, LEON, EVAN, MARK & DAVID LOBEL

best of the best exclusive

BEEF JERKY

SERVES 8

- 2 pounds flank steak, trimmed of excess fat and frozen for 1 hour
- ⅔ cup Worcestershire sauce
- ⅔ cup soy sauce
- 2 tablespoons packed dark brown sugar
- 1 teaspoon freshly ground black pepper
- ½ teaspoon onion powder
- ½ teaspoon garlic powder
- ½ teaspoon crushed red pepper

EDITOR'S NOTE
Store-bought jerky is often very dry, tough and salty. In contrast, this easy homemade jerky is delicious, with just the right amount of chewiness and an appealing sweet-salty flavor.

1. Using a very sharp knife, slice the steak across the grain ⅛ inch thick. Mix the remaining ingredients in a large bowl, add the steak slices and toss to coat. Refrigerate for 3 hours.

2. Preheat the oven to 200°F. Arrange 2 racks over 2 foil-lined baking sheets. Remove the meat from the marinade and lay the slices in a single layer on the racks. Place the baking sheets in the oven and leave the oven door slightly ajar. Cook the jerky for 3 hours, rotating the pans halfway through, until the meat is completely dry. Let cool completely before serving.

MAKE AHEAD The Beef Jerky can be stored in an airtight container for up to 2 weeks.

CHICKEN & CITRUS SLAW TOSTADAS, P. 184

COWGIRL CUISINE

PAULA DISBROWE

PUBLISHED BY WILLIAM MORROW, $29.95

It sounds like a fantasy, but it's Paula Disbrowe's real-life story: After working as a food editor at a magazine in New York City, Disbrowe moved to Rio Frio, Texas, to be the chef at Hart & Hind Fitness Ranch. Not long after, in 2005, she and her husband bought a 100-acre working ranch in Texas's Nueces Canyon. "Somewhere along the line, the Disney Texas that I first felt when I'd don a cowboy hat and pearl-snap-button shirt became more authentic," she explains. In this unique cookbook, Disbrowe shares recipes that exemplify ranch eating but with a lighter approach, like chili made with turkey, white beans and sage, and tostadas topped with shredded chicken and crunchy citrus slaw.

featured recipes Chicken & Citrus Slaw Tostadas; Ruby Salad with Crumbled Feta & Spicy Pepitas; Crostini with Lima Bean & Pecorino Puree; Turkey Chili with White Beans & Sage

best of the best exclusive Tuna & Cherry Pepper Sandwiches

Find more recipes by Paula Disbrowe at foodandwine.com/disbrowe.

CHICKEN & CITRUS SLAW TOSTADAS

SERVES 6

Vegetable oil, for frying
Six 6-inch corn tortillas
3 ounces firm tofu, diced
¼ cup fresh lime juice
2 tablespoons red wine vinegar
1 tablespoon honey
1 tablespoon Dijon mustard
1 canned chipotle chile in adobo
2 teaspoons finely grated
orange zest
1 teaspoon finely grated lime zest
Kosher salt and freshly ground
black pepper
½ small green cabbage, finely
shredded (3 cups)
¼ small red cabbage, finely
shredded (1½ cups)
1 small red onion, thinly sliced
1 large carrot, coarsely grated
3 tablespoons finely chopped
fresh cilantro
3½ cups shredded roast chicken
(from 1 medium roast chicken,
skin removed)
Lime wedges, for garnish
Additional chopped chipotle chiles in
adobo, for garnish

EDITOR'S NOTE
To save the step of frying
tortillas, substitute good-quality
store-bought tortilla chips.
Or lighten the recipe by serving
the chicken and citrus slaw in
warmed corn or wheat tortillas.

Sweet, crunchy cabbage has an affinity for a creamy, spicy dressing and bright citrus flavors. In this Mexican-inspired salad, the slaw mingles with chicken atop a crispy tostada shell. You can fry your own corn tortillas or purchase them. In this dressing, tofu fills in for mayonnaise, offering creaminess with less fat. This recipe calls for roasted, shredded chicken meat, but it's also delicious with slices of grilled chicken. Serve this salad with additional lime wedges and a bowl of chopped chipotle chiles as a garnish.

1. In a small skillet, heat ½ inch of oil over moderate heat until hot but not smoking. Add 1 tortilla and fry until golden and crisp, turning once, about 2 minutes. Transfer the tostada to paper towels to drain. Repeat with the remaining tortillas.

2. In a food processor or blender, combine the tofu with the lime juice, vinegar, honey, mustard, and chipotle and process until smooth. Add ¼ cup oil in a thin stream and process until creamy. Transfer to a bowl. Stir in the orange and lime zests and season the dressing with salt and pepper to taste.

3. In a large bowl, toss the cabbages, onion, carrot, and cilantro; season to taste with salt and pepper. Add all but 3 tablespoons of the dressing and toss. Set the tostadas on plates and mound the slaw on top. Add the chicken to the bowl, toss with the reserved 3 tablespoons of dressing, and mound on the slaw. Garnish with lime wedges and additional chipotle peppers in adobo, if desired.

RUBY SALAD WITH CRUMBLED FETA & SPICY PEPITAS

SERVES 8

TO PREPARE BEETS
1 bunch small beets (4 to 5), trimmed and scrubbed
2 to 3 fresh thyme or rosemary sprigs or 3 fresh bay leaves
½ teaspoon kosher or coarse sea salt
Olive oil

FOR THE VINAIGRETTE
1 tablespoon Dijon mustard
2 tablespoons sherry wine vinegar
2 tablespoons fresh lemon juice
Kosher salt and freshly ground black pepper
¼ cup extra-virgin olive oil

FOR THE SALAD
4 cups very thinly sliced red cabbage (1 very small head)
1 medium red onion, very thinly sliced
4 ounces (4 cups) mixed baby greens
6 ounces feta cheese, crumbled (about ½ cup)
6 ounces Spicy Pepitas (1 generous cup; recipe follows)

Several friends have told me that I'm the only person who can get them to eat beets. Since beets are one of my favorite ingredients, I consider this a major victory. Part of the trick is tempering their earthy sweetness with sharp and tangy flavors. In this salad, I rely on spicy pepitas, pungent feta cheese, and a sherry wine vinaigrette. The results are crunchy, vibrantly colored, and satisfying. For a wild color, toss the beets with the slaw and dressing ahead of time. The beet juice will stain the cabbage and onion a spectacular fuchsia. Leftovers make a very good lunch when eaten in warm corn tortillas.

1. To roast the beets, preheat the oven to 400°F. Line a rimmed baking sheet with foil. Put the beets, herbs, salt, and a drizzle of oil in the center; toss the beets to coat. Fold the foil into a loose-fitting but tightly sealed packet around the beets. Roast the packet on the baking sheet until the beets are tender, about 1 hour and 15 minutes. Let the beets cool completely in the foil. When cool, use a paring knife to peel and slice the beets into wedges (6 to 8 per beet). The beets can be roasted up to 2 days ahead and refrigerated.

2. In a small bowl, whisk together the mustard, vinegar, lemon juice, ¼ teaspoon salt, and a few grinds of pepper. Slowly whisk in the oil.

continued on p. 187

RUBY SALAD WITH CRUMBLED FETA
& SPICY PEPITAS

EDITOR'S NOTE
Shelled green pumpkin seeds, called pepitas, are available at natural-food stores and Latin markets. If you don't have time to season and roast your own, you can buy roasted, salted pepitas.

3. To assemble the salad, combine the cabbage and onion in a medium bowl and set aside. Up to an hour before serving, add the beet wedges to the cabbage and onion and gently toss with half the vinaigrette.

4. Just before serving, add the baby greens, half of the feta, and half of the pepitas; toss with the remaining vinaigrette. Arrange on a big serving platter and garnish with the remaining feta and pepitas.

Spicy Pepitas

Toss 6 ounces pepitas with 1 teaspoon corn or peanut oil, 1 teaspoon pure chile powder (such as New Mexico or ancho), and ¾ teaspoon kosher salt. Spread evenly on a rimmed baking sheet and roast at 375°F until golden and fragrant, 6 to 8 minutes (you'll hear them popping). Cool completely on the baking sheet. If making ahead, store in an airtight container.

CROSTINI WITH LIMA BEAN & PECORINO PUREE

**SERVES 6 TO 8 AS A FIRST COURSE
OR MORE AS A PARTY NIBBLE
(MAKES ABOUT 1½ CUPS PUREE)**

- 1 pound frozen Fordhook lima beans
- 2 garlic cloves
- Kosher salt
- Pinch of crushed red pepper flakes
  or 2 to 3 crumbled pequín chiles
- ½ cup grated pecorino cheese
- ½ cup coarsely chopped
  fresh mint
- 1 to 2 lemons, for juicing
- ½ cup extra-virgin olive oil
- Freshly ground black pepper

- 1 loaf Italian bread, such as
  ciabatta, thinly sliced and toasted
- 4 to 6 radishes (Icicle, French
  breakfast, or other variety),
  very thinly sliced

When I cooked in Tuscany, I fell in love with the green, garlicky fresh fava bean puree that is typically slathered over crispy rounds of crostini and served as an appetizer. Here in Texas, Fordhook lima beans have a similar taste and texture, and most important, they are available year-round in the freezer section of your grocery. This simple, unexpected appetizer is wonderful with a glass of sparkling wine like prosecco, or sauvignon blanc. A scattering of paper-thin radish slices provides a juicy crunch and brightens up the plate. If you don't have mint, you can use flat-leaf parsley or a few tablespoons of chopped fresh rosemary instead.

1. Bring a medium saucepan of salted water to a boil. Add the lima beans and cook until just tender, about 7 minutes. Drain in a colander and shock the beans in cold water. Drain again, shaking the colander to remove excess moisture.

2. Place the garlic and ½ teaspoon salt in the bowl of a food processor fitted with an electric blade and process until coarsely chopped. Add the lima beans and process until they form a rough paste. Add the red pepper flakes, pecorino, mint, and 2 tablespoons lemon juice and pulse until combined. With the motor running, add the olive oil in a steady stream until well incorporated. Taste for seasoning, adding more salt or lemon juice, and black pepper as desired.

3. To serve, slather a generous amount of puree on a slice of toasted bread and garnish with a few rounds of radish.

TURKEY CHILI WITH WHITE BEANS & SAGE

SERVES 8 TO 10

- 2 tablespoons olive oil
- 2 medium onions, chopped (about 3½ cups)
- 2 medium poblanos, chopped
- 2 celery stalks, chopped
- 2 medium carrots, chopped
- Kosher salt
- 3 pounds ground turkey (15% fat)
- Freshly ground black pepper
- 4 garlic cloves, minced
- 2 jalapeños, seeded and minced
- 24 fresh sage leaves, chopped
- 1 tablespoon plus 1 teaspoon pure chile powder (such as New Mexico or ancho)
- 1 tablespoon crumbled Mexican oregano
- 1 tablespoon plus 1 teaspoon ground cumin
- 2 teaspoons ground coriander
- 1 teaspoon Spanish smoked paprika (also called *pimentón*)
- ½ teaspoon ground allspice
- 2 bay leaves, preferably fresh
- 1 cup chopped tomatoes, with their juice
- 8 cups chicken stock
- Two 15-ounce cans cannellini or other white beans, drained
- Sour cream or plain yogurt, for garnish
- Scallions, thinly sliced, for garnish

This is a delicately seasoned chili with a thinner, fragrant broth (if you want a thicker texture, puree a cup of beans with a cup of broth). Fresh sage and Mexican oregano are delicious partners for ground turkey. Warm spices like cumin, coriander, smoked paprika, and allspice add warmth and depth to the stock. As with most stews, this is even better on the second and third days.

1. Heat the oil in a large nonstick skillet over medium-high heat. Add the onions and sauté for about 8 minutes, until softened. Add the poblanos, celery, carrots, and a pinch of salt and sauté another 10 minutes. Reduce the heat or add a small amount of water, if necessary, to prevent the vegetables from sticking or becoming too brown.

2. Place the turkey in a large pot or Dutch oven and heat over medium-high heat. Season with salt and pepper to taste and cook, stirring, until no longer pink (about 5 to 6 minutes). Add the garlic, jalapeños, sage, spices, and bay leaves and continue cooking until the meat is well coated and the spices begin to form a paste.

3. Add the sautéed vegetables, tomatoes, and chicken stock and bring the mixture to a boil. Reduce the heat and simmer, partially covered, for about 45 minutes. Add the beans and simmer 5 minutes more. Serve immediately, garnished with sour cream and scallions, or refrigerate overnight.

best of the best exclusive

TUNA & CHERRY PEPPER SANDWICHES

SERVES 4

Two 6-ounce cans Italian tuna packed in
    olive oil, drained
Four 6-inch pieces of baguette, split
¼ cup plus 2 tablespoons diced hot
    cherry peppers
Kosher salt and freshly ground pepper
Extra-virgin olive oil, for drizzling
2 hard-cooked eggs, sliced
8 basil leaves, thinly sliced
8 butter lettuce leaves

In a medium bowl, flake the tuna into small pieces. Spoon the tuna onto the bottom of the baguettes and top with the cherry peppers. Season with salt and pepper and drizzle with olive oil. Top with the egg slices and the basil and lettuce leaves, close the sandwiches and serve.

SPANISH SMOKED
PAPRIKA WINGS, P. 194

GREAT BAR FOOD AT HOME

KATE HEYHOE

PUBLISHED BY JOHN WILEY & SONS, INC., $17.95

At restaurants, chefs are teaming up with mixologists to create delectable snacks to go with inventive drinks. This is the first good book dedicated to re-creating these dishes at home—perfect for anyone who likes throwing cocktail parties. Kate Heyhoe looks around the world for inspiration: tapas bars in Spain, gastropubs in England, wine bars in Napa Valley. She gives helpful tips on pairing her recipes with different kinds of drinks, dividing the book into sections: what to eat with wine, what to eat with beer and what to eat with cocktails. The result is a fun, handy compilation of simple, irresistible snacks.

featured recipes Spanish Smoked Paprika Wings; Bursting Tomato Gratin; Chèvre-Stuffed Cornbread Kisses; Santa Fe–Caesar Crema

best of the best exclusive Pan-Fried Trout with Toasted Garlic & Lime

SPANISH SMOKED PAPRIKA WINGS

SERVES 4 AS BAR BITES

2 teaspoons ground cumin
1 teaspoon granulated (or powdered) garlic
1 teaspoon dried marjoram, crushed
1 teaspoon paprika, preferably Spanish smoked paprika
1 teaspoon salt
2 pounds chicken wing pieces
2 tablespoons olive oil

In this super-easy recipe, wing pieces roast in just a few well-chosen spices until they're golden-crisp and completely irresistible. Supermarkets sell packages of chicken wing pieces, either the center pieces or drummettes, with the tips already removed.

If you've never cooked with it before, lusty Spanish smoked paprika will change your life. Find it in specialty food stores, or order it online. I prefer the sweet, mild (rather than hot) variety for this finger-food dish, but take your pick. Even regular unsmoked paprika makes a bold statement, so don't skip over this recipe just because smoked paprika isn't handy.

1. Preheat the oven to 425°F.

2. Mix together the cumin, garlic, marjoram, paprika, and salt in a small bowl. Rinse the chicken pieces and pat dry. Rub the spice mixture all over the chicken. Pour the olive oil onto a large baking sheet and spread it around. Roll the chicken pieces in the oil until lightly coated on all sides, then arrange them neatly in a single layer without touching.

3. Bake for 20 minutes. Flip the pieces over and bake for another 20 to 25 minutes. They should be slightly crisp and golden on the outside. Serve hot or at room temperature.

BURSTING TOMATO GRATIN

SERVES 4 AS BAR BITES

 1 large egg
⅓ cup cream
 1 tablespoon all-purpose flour
 5 ounces soft goat cheese, plain or garlic and herb seasoned
1½ tablespoons fresh rosemary leaves, chopped (omit if using basil below)
 ¼ teaspoon freshly ground black pepper, or to taste
 2 tablespoons extra-virgin olive oil
 1 pound mini-tomatoes, such as grape, teardrop, or cherry tomatoes
 ½ cup chopped fresh basil (omit if using rosemary above)
 ¼ cup fine dried bread crumbs, preferably garlic-herb seasoned
 2 tablespoons freshly grated Parmesan or Romano cheese
 1 clove garlic, minced
About ¼ teaspoon salt, or to taste
Freshly ground black pepper

Besides being packed with flavor, luscious little cherry, grape, or teardrop tomatoes make this gratin a breeze. They're cooked whole, requiring no chopping, nestled under a creamy layer of goat cheese and herbs and a crunchy bread crumb topping. When you bite into the gratin, these tender tomatoes literally burst with flavor: they pop in your mouth, letting their sweet juices mingle with the tangy cheese and herbs.

The gratin may be made earlier in the day and served at room temperature, or reheated. You can also prepare the creamy cheese mixture a day in advance; then on serving day, simply pour the tomatoes into a glass baking dish with some olive oil, cover with the cheese mixture and bread crumbs, and bake, slice, and serve. Voilà! Elegant little bar plates for very little effort.

1. Preheat the oven to 425°F.

2. In a small mixing bowl, beat the egg until mixed. Beat in the cream and flour. Mash in the goat cheese, rosemary, if using, and pepper, until the mixture is well combined and creamy. If the mixture is too thick, blend in more cream: the mixture should be moist and easily spreadable, like a cream cheese frosting. (This can be made a day in advance and refrigerated.)

continued on p. 196

3. Pour 1 tablespoon olive oil into a shallow baking dish just big enough to hold the tomatoes in a single layer (a ceramic tart pan or glass pie pan works best). Add the tomatoes, rolling them around so the oil coats them as well as the bottom and sides of the dish. Stir in the basil, if using. (You can prepare this step earlier in the day, but chop and add the basil just before cooking.)

4. Mix together the bread crumbs, Parmesan or Romano, garlic, salt, and pepper to taste. Sprinkle half of this mixture on the tomatoes.

5. Gently spoon the goat cheese mixture over the tomatoes and crumbs, distributing it evenly. Top with the remaining bread crumb mixture and drizzle the remaining tablespoon of olive oil on top.

6. Bake until the tomatoes soften but have not yet burst, 15 to 18 minutes. The top should be golden brown, but if not, finish the gratin under the broiler for a few seconds. Slice the gratin into wedges and serve hot or at room temperature, with small forks (or reheat in a 375°F oven for about 5 minutes).

CHÈVRE-STUFFED
CORNBREAD KISSES

MAKES 24 MINI-MUFFINS

3 ounces goat cheese
3 ounces cream cheese
 with chives
1 cup yellow cornmeal
1 cup all-purpose flour
⅓ cup granulated sugar
1 tablespoon baking
 powder
1 teaspoon salt
1 cup buttermilk
⅓ cup vegetable oil
1 large egg

These tiny, golden cornbread muffins may look traditional, but they're filled with a tangy white cloud of goat cheese and cream cheese, enhanced by chives. Fill greased mini-muffin tins (with muffins 1¾ to 2 inches in diameter, twelve muffins per tin) directly with the batter; the crust is better when they're baked in the muffin tin rather than in paper liners.

1. Preheat the oven to 375°F. Generously grease 2 mini-muffin tins.

2. In a small bowl, blend together the goat cheese and cream cheese with a fork.

3. Combine the cornmeal, flour, sugar, baking powder, and salt in a mixing bowl. Measure the buttermilk and oil into a measuring cup and add the egg. Beat lightly with a fork until blended. Pour the liquid ingredients into the dry ingredients. Mix just until blended.

4. Fill the muffin cups about half full. Spoon a lump of the cheese mixture into each muffin. Top each muffin with the remaining batter—it's okay if some of the cheese pokes through the batter. Bake about 15 minutes, or until the edges are golden brown. Let the muffins cool in the pans about 10 minutes before removing. Serve warm or at room temperature.

SANTA FE–CAESAR CREMA

MAKES ABOUT 1½ CUPS

- 2 cloves garlic
- ½ cup packed fresh cilantro
- 3 canned anchovy fillets, or to taste
- 1 large ripe avocado
- 2 tablespoons fresh lime juice
- 2 tablespoons fresh lemon juice
- ½ cup regular or low-fat sour cream
- ¼ cup finely grated Parmesan cheese
- 1 teaspoon extra-virgin olive oil
- ¼ teaspoon Worcestershire sauce

Coarsely ground black pepper

This lively avocado mixture can be a dip or a spread, depending on how you use it. Set a small bowl of it out with bagel chips, garlic toasts, or small romaine leaves, or spoon it over taquitos or mini-tacos. It's got the spirit of old Santa Fe with the flavor punch of a Caesar salad.

1. With the food processor running, peel and drop the garlic cloves, cilantro, and anchovies into the feed tube and process until the garlic is finely chopped. Cut open the avocado and scoop the flesh into the food processor bowl. Pour the lime and lemon juices and sour cream over the avocado. Pulse just long enough to mix up the avocado (chunks are okay; contact with the acids helps prevent the avocado from turning brown).

2. Add the Parmesan, olive oil, and Worcestershire. Pulse until well blended with little green cilantro flecks. Taste to correct the seasonings. Garnish with pepper. Serve now or refrigerate to serve later or the next day. Bring to room temperature for fullest flavor. (The crema will last 3 days, but the flavors will diminish over time.)

best of the best exclusive

PAN-FRIED TROUT WITH TOASTED GARLIC & LIME

SERVES 4

16 large garlic cloves, unpeeled
¼ cup plus 2 tablespoons fresh lime juice
4 whole rainbow trout (about 3 pounds total), cleaned
1 tablespoon plus 1 teaspoon ground cumin
1 tablespoon kosher salt
¼ cup extra-virgin olive oil
Lime wedges, for serving

EDITOR'S NOTE

This recipe will appear in Heyhoe's next cookbook, *New Green Basics*, which focuses on sustainable ingredients and kitchen practices. She favors rainbow trout for its mild, distinctive flavor, and adds that it's a very eco-friendly fish. For more environmental tips and recipes, check out Heyhoe's websites, globalgourmet.com and newgreenbasics.com.

1. Bring a small saucepan of water to a boil. Add the garlic and cook until the skins begin to shrivel, about 3 minutes. Drain. Peel the garlic cloves and halve them lengthwise.

2. Pour the lime juice into a large, shallow bowl or glass pie plate. Dip the trout in the lime juice on all sides, until coated inside and out. Season the fish with the cumin and salt.

3. In each of 2 large nonstick skillets, heat 2 tablespoons of olive oil until shimmering. Add the trout and cook over moderately high heat until the skin is golden and crisp, about 5 minutes. Turn the fish and add the garlic to the skillet. Cook, stirring the garlic occasionally, until the fish is cooked through and the garlic is golden, about 5 minutes. Remove the garlic when it is golden even if the fish has not finished cooking. Transfer the trout to plates and spoon some of the garlic on top. Serve with lime wedges.

CRAB-CORN CAKES WITH
BASIL-JALAPEÑO SAUCE, P. 202

THE DEEN BROS. COOKBOOK

JAMIE & BOBBY DEEN & MELISSA CLARK

PUBLISHED BY MEREDITH BOOKS, $24.95

This collection of recipes, mainly from small-town, family-run businesses—bakeries, diners, pretzel joints, pork stores, barbecue spots, candy companies—is an excellent sampling of homespun American food today. The authors are Jamie and Bobby Deen, hosts of a Food Network show called *Road Tasted* and sons of Food Network celebrity Paula Deen. On the show, the Deens taste local specialties from around the country. Here, they present pure crowd-pleasers inspired by their travels, from Seattle to Texas to the Bronx: crab-corn cakes, bacony shrimp salad sandwiches and chocolate chip pie with chocolate chip whipped cream.

featured recipes Crab-Corn Cakes with Basil-Jalapeño Sauce; The Deen Brothers' BBQ Chicken; Shrimp Salad Sandwiches; Chocolate Chip Pie

best of the best exclusive Zesty Grilled Pork Chops with Pineapple Salsa

CRAB-CORN CAKES
WITH BASIL-JALAPEÑO SAUCE

SERVES 6

CRAB CAKES

3	tablespoons unsalted butter
4	scallions, trimmed and finely chopped
1	clove garlic, minced
1	pound crab claw meat
½	cup frozen corn, thawed
½	cup dried bread crumbs
1	egg
3	tablespoons mayonnaise
1	tablespoon Dijon mustard
2	teaspoons chopped fresh parsley leaves

Freshly ground black pepper

2	tablespoons vegetable oil
⅓	cup yellow cornmeal

BASIL-JALAPEÑO TARTAR SAUCE

½	cup mayonnaise
1	jalapeño, seeded and finely chopped
1	clove garlic, minced
2	tablespoons chopped fresh basil leaves
2	teaspoons capers, drained and chopped
1½	teaspoons freshly squeezed lemon juice

Pinch salt

Freshly ground black pepper

EDITOR'S NOTE

These sweet, meaty crab cakes were even better with a pinch of kosher salt.

We put our own spin on crab cakes by adding corn and plenty of flavorful ingredients, including scallions and mustard. Then we top the crispy cakes with a savory, herby tartar sauce.

1. In a medium skillet, heat 1 tablespoon of the butter over medium-high heat. Add the scallions and garlic. Cook and stir for 2 to 3 minutes or until softened. Place the mixture in a large bowl. Add the crabmeat, corn, bread crumbs, egg, mayonnaise, mustard, parsley, and pepper to taste; mix well. Divide the mixture into 12 portions and form into ½-inch-thick patties. Place the patties on a baking sheet and chill for 1 hour.

2. Meanwhile, in a small bowl, stir together all of the tartar sauce ingredients. Refrigerate until ready to use.

3. Preheat oven to 375°F. In a large skillet, heat the remaining 2 tablespoons butter and the oil over medium-high heat. Dredge each crab cake in the cornmeal, turning to coat evenly. Sear the cakes for 3 to 4 minutes per side or until golden brown. Return the crab cakes to the baking sheet. Bake for 10 minutes. Serve the crab cakes hot with Basil-Jalapeño Tartar Sauce.

THE DEEN BROTHERS' BBQ CHICKEN

SERVES 3 TO 4

- 1 cup ketchup
- ¼ cup packed dark brown sugar
- 2 tablespoons orange juice
- 1 teaspoon Worcestershire sauce
- 1 teaspoon liquid smoke
- ½ teaspoon dry mustard powder
- ¼ teaspoon cayenne pepper
- One 3½-pound chicken, cut into 8 pieces

1. Preheat oven to 375°F or prepare a grill (brush the grill grate lightly with oil).

2. In a large bowl, stir together all ingredients except the chicken. Reserve ⅓ cup of the barbecue sauce; set aside. Add the chicken to the remaining sauce in the bowl, turning to coat.

3. Arrange the coated chicken in a roasting pan or on the grill. Cook (covered, if grilling) for 40 to 45 minutes or until cooked through, basting with the reserved ⅓ cup sauce after 20 minutes.

SHRIMP SALAD SANDWICHES

SERVES 4

½ cup mayonnaise
1 tablespoon freshly squeezed lemon juice
1 to 2 pickled jalapeños, seeded and finely chopped
1 pound cooked and peeled shrimp, coarsely chopped
8 slices bacon, cooked and crumbled
Salt and freshly ground black pepper
8 slices challah bread, toasted
4 leaves red leaf lettuce
4 slices tomato (8 slices if tomatoes are small)

Royers Round Top Cafe [in Round Top, Texas] serves some pretty gourmet food, like shrimp BLTs on jalapeño sourdough. Just as intriguing is our sandwich, where flavorful fresh shrimp get spruced up with bacon, jalapeños, and a lemony mayo dressing.

1. In a medium bowl, stir together the mayonnaise, lemon juice, and jalapeño. Add the shrimp and bacon; toss to combine. Season to taste with salt and pepper.

2. Spread the shrimp salad evenly on 4 slices of bread. Top with lettuce, tomato, and the remaining slices of bread.

CHOCOLATE CHIP PIE

SERVES 12 TO 16

PIES

2¾ cups all-purpose flour
1½ teaspoons salt
1¼ teaspoons baking soda
1 teaspoon baking powder
1 cup (2 sticks) unsalted butter, softened
1½ cups packed light brown sugar
½ cup granulated sugar
3 large eggs
1 tablespoon vanilla
3 cups semisweet chocolate chips
2 cups chopped walnuts (optional)

WHIPPED CREAM

2 pints (4 cups) heavy cream
¼ cup confectioners' (powdered) sugar
½ cup miniature semisweet chocolate chips

EDITOR'S NOTE

In place of whipped cream, you can top these pies with softened ice cream (we like vanilla or mint chocolate chip), then freeze the pies until the ice cream is firm enough to slice.

1. Preheat oven to 350°F. Grease two 9-inch pie plates; set aside.

2. In a large bowl, sift together the flour, salt, baking soda, and baking powder. In the bowl of an electric mixer, cream together the butter, brown sugar, and granulated sugar. Add the eggs, one at a time, beating until incorporated. Beat in the vanilla. Add the flour mixture, a little at a time, and mix until fully combined. Fold in the 3 cups chocolate chips and, if desired, the walnuts. Divide the dough between the prepared pie plates and smooth the tops with a spatula.

3. Bake about 30 minutes or until the pies are golden and slightly firm to the touch but still soft. If the pies begin to darken too much before they are baked through, cover with foil and continue baking. Let the pies cool completely on a wire rack.

4. While the pies cool, whip the cream until soft peaks form (tips curl). Add the confectioners' sugar and whip until just combined. Fold in the chocolate chips. Refrigerate the whipped cream until ready to use. Spread the whipped cream over the pies and serve.

best of the best exclusive

ZESTY GRILLED PORK CHOPS WITH PINEAPPLE SALSA

SERVES 6

¼ cup plus 2 tablespoons extra-virgin olive oil

1 teaspoon finely grated orange zest

¼ cup plus 2 tablespoons fresh orange juice

1 tablespoon finely grated fresh ginger

1 teaspoon hot sauce

Salt and freshly ground pepper

Six ½-inch-thick boneless pork chops (1¾ pounds total)

½ medium pineapple—peeled, cored and cut into ¼-inch dice (about 2 cups)

1 tomato, seeded and cut into ¼-inch dice

1 small red bell pepper, seeded and cut into ¼-inch dice

½ small white onion, cut into ¼-inch dice

1 jalapeño, seeded and minced

1 tablespoon minced cilantro leaves

1 teaspoon sugar

EDITOR'S NOTE
The Deen brothers insist that there's nothing better alongside these super-juicy pork chops than white rice and black beans.

1. In a large glass baking dish, whisk the olive oil with the orange zest, orange juice, ginger, hot sauce, 1 teaspoon of salt and ¼ teaspoon of pepper. Add the pork chops and turn to coat. Let the chops marinate at room temperature for 1 hour, turning once.

2. Meanwhile, in a medium bowl, mix the pineapple with the tomato, bell pepper, onion, jalapeño, cilantro and sugar. Season the pineapple salsa with salt and pepper.

3. Light a grill or preheat a grill pan. Remove the pork chops from the marinade and grill over moderately high heat, turning once, until just cooked through, about 7 minutes total. Transfer the pork chops to plates. Spoon some of the pineapple salsa on top and serve.

MAKE AHEAD The pineapple salsa can be refrigerated for up to 2 days.

MAPLE-GLAZED RIBS, P. 210

COOKING WITH SHELBURNE FARMS

MELISSA PASANEN WITH RICK GENCARELLI

PUBLISHED BY VIKING STUDIO, $34.95

This book is a celebration of the singular mission of Shelburne Farms: to cultivate a conservation ethic. Shelburne Farms, located on 1,400 acres in Shelburne, Vermont, is a working farm and education center with a historic inn and restaurant. The farm's bakery, dairy (with grass-fed cows) and market garden are all intended to help teach people how to create a sustainable future. In *Cooking with Shelburne Farms,* the inn's chef, Rick Gencarelli, offers simple, enticing recipes arranged into chapters based on Vermont's iconic ingredients, including milk and cheese, root-cellar vegetables, wild mushrooms, apples and maple syrup. There are also lovely profiles of the artisans associated with Shelburne Farms, among them the apple grower, the vegetable farmer and the cheesemaker.

featured recipes Maple-Glazed Ribs; Mushroom & Root Vegetable Potpie; Grilled Steak with Cumin-Coriander Mushrooms; Cider-Glazed Squash & Arugula Salad

best of the best exclusive Green Bean Salad with Bacon & Tarragon

MAPLE-GLAZED RIBS

SERVES 4 TO 6

 2 tablespoons garlic powder
2½ tablespoons coarse kosher salt
 1 tablespoon mustard powder,
   such as Colman's
 3 packed tablespoons light
   brown sugar
 2 tablespoons plus 1 teaspoon
   smoked sweet Spanish paprika
   or sweet paprika
 4 pounds baby back ribs
 ½ cup beer, preferably an amber ale
   (see Before You Start)
 ½ cup maple syrup, Grade B for
   strongest flavor
 ¼ cup cider vinegar
 ¼ cup ketchup

Although Rick doesn't have much opportunity to serve ribs at the Inn, they are one of his favorite things to make for friends and family, and he is quite an expert on different styles of barbecue. He would slow-cook these in his kettle grill, but the oven makes them much easier and more predictable. This recipe makes a sweet, sticky rib—not the wet, sloppy kind.

BEFORE YOU START Ideally, you would rub the ribs ahead of time and let them absorb the flavors for at least an hour, but the recipe works well even without doing that. Using smoked sweet Spanish paprika brings a wonderful smokiness to these ribs, but they will be delicious with regular paprika too. You can find smoked sweet paprika in some specialty markets. We like Vermont's Long Trail amber ale in the mop—and to drink with the ribs too.

1. Preheat the oven to 325°F. In a small bowl, whisk together the garlic powder, salt, mustard powder, brown sugar, and 2 tablespoons of the paprika. Set aside about 1½ tablespoons of the rub, and rub the rest over both sides of the ribs.

2. With the meaty side down, wrap each rack of ribs in foil like a package. Place them on a rimmed cookie sheet or shallow roasting pan. Cook for about 2 hours until the meat is very tender.

EDITOR'S NOTE

Maple syrup is graded by color and flavor. Grade A syrup (which is further broken down into light, medium and dark amber) is relatively light and delicate, and is best used for drizzling. Grade B syrup is heavier, with a stronger maple flavor; it's ideal for cooking.

3. Increase the oven temperature to 450°F with a rack in the second-highest position. Unwrap the ribs carefully, pour off and discard any accumulated fat, and replace the ribs on the foil in the pan.

4. In a small saucepan, whisk together the beer, maple syrup, and cider vinegar. Using a basting brush or crumpled paper towel, mop both sides of the ribs well with the mixture, finishing with the meaty side up. Reserve the remaining mop.

5. Sprinkle the reserved rub over the meaty side of the ribs and cook them in the oven for about 10 minutes until glazed and crusty.

6. While the ribs are finishing, whisk the remaining 1 teaspoon of paprika and the ketchup into the reserved mop. Simmer it over medium heat for 5 to 7 minutes until slightly thickened. Adjust seasoning to taste and serve with the ribs.

MUSHROOM & ROOT VEGETABLE POTPIE

SERVES 8 TO 10

Cheddar & Herb Biscuits (recipe follows), made with fresh thyme and cut into twelve 2-inch rounds

3 pounds assorted root vegetables, such as carrots, turnips, rutabagas, beets, parsnips, and sweet potatoes, peeled and cut into 1-inch cubes

3 tablespoons olive oil

1 tablespoon coarsely chopped fresh thyme leaves

1½ teaspoons coarse kosher salt plus more to taste

Freshly ground black pepper to taste

6 tablespoons unsalted butter

3 medium leeks, white and light green parts only, halved lengthwise, thinly sliced, and rinsed thoroughly

2 pounds mixed mushrooms, quartered or torn into bite-size pieces (see Before You Start)

3 tablespoons all-purpose flour

4 cups mushroom stock or vegetable stock (see Before You Start)

A satisfying stew of meaty mushrooms and sweet, roasted root vegetables. The Cheddar & Herb Biscuits are a great topper and make this our homage to the chicken pies served at church suppers all over Vermont, which are always finished with fluffy biscuits baked on top.

BEFORE YOU START This dish can take a wide variety of mushrooms and, in fact, works best with a variety of those on the sturdy side, such as cultivated cremini and white buttons as well as wild pheasant back, thin slices of chicken mushrooms, and a mixture of gilled mushrooms. If you cannot find prepackaged mushroom stock—which is available in some supermarkets and natural foods stores either in concentrate or in cartons—warm the vegetable stock and soak one ounce of your choice of dried mushrooms in it for about 20 minutes. Finely mince the reconstituted dried mushrooms and add them to the sautéed mushroom-leek mixture with the stock. The filling must be hot when you put the biscuits on it, or the biscuit bottoms will get gummy.

1. Make the Cheddar & Herb Biscuits, but do not brush them with the buttermilk yet. Cover the biscuits with a damp towel and refrigerate.

2. Preheat the oven to 400°F. Toss together the root vegetables in a 9 by 13-inch baking dish with 2 tablespoons of the olive oil, the thyme, 1 teaspoon of the salt, and pepper to taste. Roast for 40 to 45 minutes, or until a fork easily pierces a piece of each vegetable. (Some may be softer than others.) Take the vegetables out of the oven and increase the heat to 425°F.

EDITOR'S NOTE
To make individual potpies,
spoon the filling into
ramekins, top each with
a biscuit and bake.

3. While the root vegetables are roasting, set a large sauté pan or skillet over medium-high heat and melt 1 tablespoon of the butter until foamy. Add the leeks and cook, stirring occasionally, until softened, about 3 to 4 minutes.

4. Add the mushrooms to the pan along with the remaining tablespoon of olive oil, starting with the most sturdy varieties and sprinkling them with the remaining ½ teaspoon of salt. Give them about a 5-minute head start, and then add more delicate varieties. Cook, stirring occasionally, until the mushrooms have given up their liquid and turned golden and they make a squeaking noise against the pan, up to an additional 10 to 12 minutes.

5. Reduce the heat to medium and add the remaining 5 tablespoons of butter to the pan. When the butter has melted, stir in the flour and cook for 1 to 2 minutes until the flour is golden. Stir in the mushroom stock and bring to a simmer. Cook, stirring, for 4 to 5 minutes, until the gravy thickens. Adjust seasoning to taste.

6. Pour the mushroom gravy over the roasted root vegetables in the baking dish and stir to combine. Arrange the prepared biscuits on top of the hot filling. Brush the biscuits with buttermilk. Bake for 15 to 20 minutes until the biscuits are golden brown and the filling is bubbly.

PREPARE-AHEAD TIP You can prepare the filling up to 24 hours ahead and keep it in the refrigerator. Warm the filling, covered with foil, in a 425°F oven for 30 minutes before adding the biscuits.

continued on p. 214

- 3 cups all-purpose flour
- 2 tablespoons baking powder
- ½ teaspoon baking soda
- 1 teaspoon table salt
- 6 tablespoons cold unsalted butter, cut into small bits
- 1 cup (about 4 ounces) grated cheddar
- 2 tablespoons chopped fresh thyme, sage, or rosemary leaves
- 1¼ cups cold buttermilk plus a little more to brush the biscuit tops

Cheddar & Herb Biscuits

Nothing beats a good biscuit, especially if it is golden and fragrant with cheddar and fresh herbs. These are wonderful with soup, with stews, or as a topping for potpies like our Mushroom & Root Vegetable Potpie.

BEFORE YOU START Go for an aged sharp cheddar like one- or two-year Shelburne Farms. The key to light and flaky biscuits is to keep the ingredients as cold as possible and to work the dough as little as possible. Rick and I experienced proof of this when we mixed and rolled out multiple batches of biscuits in the unheated, off-season Inn kitchen in January. We were a little chilly, but the biscuits were perfect.

1. Preheat the oven to 425°F. In a large bowl, whisk together the flour, baking powder, baking soda, and salt.

2. With your fingers or two forks, work the butter into the flour mixture until the dough looks like fine gravel with a few larger butter bumps throughout. (Alternatively, use a food processor with a few short pulses.) Stir in the cheddar and thyme. Add the buttermilk gradually, just until a pinch of dough comes together when you squeeze it between your fingers.

3. Lightly flour the counter and dump the dough onto it. Knead it a few times to bring it together and then use a lightly floured rolling pin to roll the dough out ¾ inch thick. Cut out the biscuits with a 2½-inch cutter or a glass. (You can reroll scraps once but not more or the biscuits will be tough.)

4. Place the biscuits on an ungreased cookie sheet and brush the tops with buttermilk. Bake for 15 to 20 minutes, until golden brown.

GRILLED STEAK WITH CUMIN-CORIANDER MUSHROOMS

SERVES 4

2 tablespoons whole coriander seeds

1 tablespoon whole cumin seeds

Freshly ground black pepper to taste

1 tablespoon minced garlic
   (about 3 cloves)

2 skirt steaks, about 1½ to
   2 pounds total

1½ teaspoons coarse kosher salt
   plus more to taste

3 tablespoons olive oil plus more
   as needed

¾ pound mixed mushrooms
   (see Before You Start)

2 teaspoons freshly squeezed
   lemon juice

Parsley Sauce (recipe follows) if desired

This is a quick, easy recipe that is most rewarding when made with a variety of mushrooms. British food writer Elizabeth David inspired the coriander seasoning, for which mushrooms have a wonderful affinity. Serve the steak and mushrooms on a bed of arugula or baby spinach leaves.

BEFORE YOU START You can use almost any mix of wild or exotic cultivated mushrooms as long as they are not too delicate. Larger pieces of oyster mushrooms, honeys, pig's ear *Gomphus,* and slices of hen of the woods work well. Skirt steak is a very reasonably priced cut of steak that has recently become more widely available in supermarkets thanks to the fact that it is used for fajitas. It is flavorful, lean, and very thin. It cooks in a flash and becomes tough if overcooked, so do not even think about taking it past medium. As Rick says, "This is a meat-eater's meat." Flank steak can be used instead, but since it's thicker, it will take a little longer to cook.

1. Prepare a gas or charcoal grill to cook over medium-high heat. Alternatively, place a large broiler-proof skillet, preferably cast iron, on the oven rack in the second-highest position, about 4 to 5 inches from the heating element. Preheat the broiler on its highest setting for at least 15 minutes.

continued on p. 217

GRILLED STEAK WITH
CUMIN-CORIANDER MUSHROOMS

2. With a mortar and pestle or a spice grinder, crush the coriander and cumin seeds together. Add about 10 grinds of pepper to the mixture and stir in the minced garlic. Take 2 teaspoons of the rub and set it aside.

3. Lay the skirt steaks on a platter and slice them into pieces that will be manageable on the grill. (Generally, each steak will do best cut into two long pieces of about 8 to 12 inches.) Sprinkle the steaks well with 1 teaspoon of the salt, and then apply the rub evenly on both sides of the steaks. Drizzle them evenly with 1 tablespoon of the olive oil and rub it in with your fingers. Set aside.

4. Tear the mushrooms into bite-size pieces or slice caps into ¼-inch slices, leaving smaller ones whole.

5. In a large skillet or sauté pan, heat the remaining 2 tablespoons of olive oil over medium-high heat for about 2 minutes. Add the mushrooms to the pan, along with the remaining ½ teaspoon salt and reserved 2 teaspoons of the rub. Cook, stirring occasionally, until the mushrooms have given up their liquid and turned golden and they make a squeaking noise against the pan, 10 to 12 minutes. Stir in the lemon juice and cover the pot to keep the mushrooms warm while grilling the steak.

6. Grill or broil the steak for 4 to 5 minutes per side. Let the steak rest for 10 minutes, loosely covered with foil to keep it warm. Slice the steak very thinly across the grain and serve it topped with the mushrooms and Parsley Sauce if desired.

continued on p. 218

SERVES 4

3 tablespoons freshly squeezed
   lemon juice
¼ teaspoon ground cumin
¼ teaspoon ground coriander
½ teaspoon coarse kosher salt
   plus more to taste
¼ cup olive oil
½ cup finely chopped fresh
   flat-leaf parsley
2 large shallots, finely minced, or
   ¼ cup finely minced red onion

EDITOR'S NOTE

At Shelburne Farms, this lemony,
fresh-tasting sauce is also served
with fried pork chops. It's wonderful
with fish, too, especially a variety
like salmon or swordfish that isn't
too delicate to stand up to the deep
flavors of cumin and coriander.

Parsley Sauce

In a small bowl, whisk the lemon juice with the cumin,
coriander, and salt. Whisk the olive oil in slowly, and then stir
in the parsley and shallots. Adjust seasoning to taste.

CIDER-GLAZED SQUASH
& ARUGULA SALAD

SERVES 4 TO 6

1 butternut squash (3 pounds) or pie pumpkin (4 pounds), peeled and seeded, flesh cut into about 20 ¾-inch cubes (see Before You Start)
1 tablespoon olive oil
2 tablespoons apple cider or natural apple juice
½ teaspoon coarse kosher salt
20 raw, peeled hazelnuts
Cider Vinaigrette (recipe follows)
4 cups (5 to 6 ounces) baby arugula
½ cup (about 2 to 3 ounces) crumbled fresh goat cheese

This salad is modeled after Rick's popular and very pretty Harvest Salad. Since arugula is one of the hardier greens from the Market Garden, it survives early frosts and carries through to the very end of the season. Its bite provides the perfect foil for the dense, sweet cubes of squash. The cider-glazed squash also makes a nice side dish in its own right.

BEFORE YOU START After you've cut your nice, even cubes of squash, you will have some perfectly edible bits left over. See the Variation below for ways to use them.

1. Preheat the oven to 400°F. In a shallow roasting pan or rimmed cookie sheet, toss the squash with the olive oil, apple cider, and salt. Roast the squash for 20 to 25 minutes, turning once, until it is starting to color and all the liquid has evaporated. Cool the squash.

2. While the squash is roasting, coarsely chop the hazelnuts and put them in the oven in a small baking dish next to the squash to toast for about 10 to 12 minutes until golden and fragrant. Make the vinaigrette.

3. Arrange the arugula on a platter and toss it with about ⅓ cup of the vinaigrette. Top with the cider-glazed squash cubes, crumbled goat cheese, and toasted hazelnuts and drizzle with a little more vinaigrette as desired.

VARIATION Try the cider-glazed squash or any leftover squash bits roasted up the same way, tossed with pasta, pearl barley, or wheat berries and some wilted arugula or baby spinach. Top with goat cheese and the toasted hazelnuts.

continued on p. 220

PREPARE-AHEAD TIP The squash can be roasted up to a day ahead and kept in the refrigerator. Bring to room temperature before serving. The hazelnuts can be toasted ahead and, after cooling, kept sealed at room temperature for a few days.

Cider Vinaigrette

MAKES 1 CUP

½ cup apple cider or
    natural apple juice
2 tablespoons cider vinegar
1 teaspoon pure maple syrup,
    Grade B for strongest flavor
1 shallot, finely minced
½ teaspoon coarse kosher salt
    plus more to taste
¼ cup olive oil
Freshly ground black pepper to taste

EDITOR'S NOTE
This fruity vinaigrette is on the sweet side. If you prefer a tangier dressing, simply reduce the amount of apple cider or juice to ⅓ cup.

This vinaigrette features two of Vermont's signature flavors and graces many fall salads at the Inn, including the Cider-Glazed Squash & Arugula Salad. Rick also uses it with another wonderful combination: arugula with thinly sliced Shelburne Orchards Cortland apples (they and Empires would both work well because they don't turn brown as soon as they are cut), spiced maple nuts, and thin shavings of Shelburne Farms' prized clothbound cheddar. Or try the dressing over baby spinach leaves, golden raisins, toasted slivered almonds, and a little fresh goat cheese.

BEFORE YOU START When Rick makes this dressing at the Inn, he reduces the apple cider slowly on the stove by about half to intensify it; you're welcome to do that, but we like it just fine without that time-consuming step.

1. In a blender or mini food processor, blend together the cider, cider vinegar, maple syrup, shallot, and salt.

2. Gradually add the olive oil and blend to emulsify. Adjust seasoning to taste.

best of the best exclusive

GREEN BEAN SALAD WITH BACON & TARRAGON

SERVES 4

1   pound green beans
8   thick slices of bacon (½ pound),
      cut crosswise into ½-inch strips
2   tablespoons extra-virgin
      olive oil
1½ tablespoons fresh lemon juice
1   teaspoon kosher salt
20 grape tomatoes (5½ ounces), halved
½   small red onion, halved and
      thinly sliced
¼   cup tarragon leaves, finely chopped
Freshly ground pepper

1. Bring a large pot of salted water to a boil. Fill a large bowl with ice water. Cook the green beans in the boiling water until crisp-tender, about 3 minutes. Using a slotted spoon, transfer the green beans to the ice water bath to chill, about 3 minutes. Drain the green beans and pat dry with paper towels.

2. In a large skillet, cook the bacon over moderate heat until crisp, about 10 minutes. Using a slotted spoon, transfer the bacon to paper towels to drain. Reserve 1 tablespoon of the bacon fat.

3. In a large bowl, whisk the reserved bacon fat with the olive oil, lemon juice and salt. Add the green beans, bacon, tomatoes, onion and tarragon to the dressing in the bowl and toss to coat. Season with pepper and serve.

BAKING

NOT-SO-ANGELIC ANGEL PIE, P. 226

STICKY, CHEWY, MESSY, GOOEY

JILL O'CONNOR

PUBLISHED BY CHRONICLE BOOKS, $22.95

Jill O'Connor's passion for sweets comes from books. As a child, she fantasized about Winnie the Pooh's sticky honey pot and Laura Ingalls Wilder's horehound candy. As an adult, she creates recipes that evoke a child's playfulness. O'Connor encourages the reader to "fearlessly enter my world of chocolate, butterscotch, and marshmallows with a gutsy, guilt-free, take-no-prisoners sense of abandon, ready to trek through these sugar-speckled, cream-drenched pages to find your favorites." Her Quicky Sticky Biscuits are brilliantly simple and—as the book's title promises—wonderfully sticky and gooey; her banana bread pudding, made with toasted buttered brioche and topped with hot fudge sauce, is warm and luscious.

featured recipes Not-So-Angelic Angel Pie; Banana Bread Pudding with Hot Fudge & Toasted Walnuts; All-Grown-Up S'mores; Quicky Sticky Biscuits

best of the best exclusive Coconut Shortbread Cookies

NOT-SO-ANGELIC ANGEL PIE

SERVES 8

Cornstarch for sprinkling

FOR THE PIE SHELL
- ¾ cup graham cracker crumbs
- 1 cup finely chopped walnuts or pecans, toasted
- 5 ounces semisweet chocolate, very finely chopped
- 6 large egg whites, at room temperature
- ½ teaspoon cream of tartar
- ⅛ teaspoon salt
- 2 cups granulated sugar
- 1 teaspoon pure vanilla extract

FOR THE FILLING
- 2 cups heavy cream, chilled
- ⅔ cup confectioners' sugar, sifted
- 1 teaspoon pure vanilla extract
- 3 cups fresh strawberries, hulled and halved, or fresh raspberries

My friend Debby Jo Jones taught me how to make Angel Pie at Mountain Meadow Ranch, the one summer we were there together. She was the dinner cook, and cool as a cucumber, even under pressure. Her food was delicious, from her corn fritters to this chewy, nutty, chocolate-studded meringue dessert filled with whipped cream and strawberries.

Line a large baking sheet (not an air-cushioned one) with parchment paper and sprinkle lightly with cornstarch. Set aside. Preheat the oven to 350°F.

TO MAKE THE PIE SHELL In a large bowl, stir together the graham cracker crumbs, nuts, and chocolate until completely combined. Set aside.

In another bowl, using an electric mixer set at low speed, beat the egg whites and cream of tartar until foamy. Add the salt, increase the speed to medium-high, and continue beating until soft peaks form. Continue beating, adding the sugar to the egg whites 1 tablespoon at a time until stiff, glossy peaks form. Beat in the vanilla.

Fold a large dollop of the egg whites into the crumb mixture to lighten it. Gently fold the remaining egg whites into the crumb mixture just until combined, being careful not to deflate them. Do not overmix.

Spoon the entire mixture onto the baking sheet and, using a metal spatula, quickly spread into an 8- to 10-inch round. Bake until the pie is puffy and golden with a crisp outer shell, 25 to 30 minutes. Transfer to a wire rack and let cool completely.

TO MAKE THE FILLING Combine the chilled cream, ⅓ cup of the confectioners' sugar, and the vanilla in a bowl. Using an electric mixer set at medium speed, beat until the cream holds firm peaks.

When ready to serve, carefully peel the pie shell from the parchment and place on a serving plate. Fill the center of the shell with the whipped cream. Mix the strawberries with the remaining ⅓ cup confectioners' sugar and pile on top of the cream. Cut into wedges and serve immediately.

BANANA BREAD PUDDING WITH HOT FUDGE & TOASTED WALNUTS

- 1 loaf brioche (13 ounces), cut crosswise into 12 slices about 1 inch thick
- ¾ cup (1½ sticks) unsalted butter, melted, plus 2 tablespoons cold butter, cut into little bits
- 1½ cups sugar
- 1 tablespoon ground cinnamon
- 8 large eggs
- 3 large egg yolks
- 1 teaspoon pure vanilla extract
- 2 cups heavy cream
- 1 cup whole milk
- ⅛ teaspoon salt
- 1 cup mashed ripe bananas
- My Favorite Ganache (recipe follows)
- 1 cup coarsely chopped walnuts, toasted
- Vanilla ice cream or sweetened whipped cream for serving (optional)

EDITOR'S NOTE

There's no need to use up all the melted butter called for here—just use what you need for brushing the pan and brioche slices. You're likely to have some left over, which you can refrigerate and remelt for another use.

My husband, Jim, tasted banana bread pudding at one of his favorite San Francisco restaurants and raved about it for months. He asked me to duplicate it and finally I relented. When he said "banana bread pudding," I thought he meant a bread pudding made with banana bread. Not exactly what he had in mind. His response was less than enthusiastic, and I realized you can't have a thin skin when testing new recipes. My second attempt, however, hit the mark: a cream-rich, eggy custard spiked with ripe bananas and combined with fat cubes of cinnamon-toasted, buttery brioche. Heaven for banana—and comfort food—lovers alike. It only gets better when drizzled with warm, dark chocolate sauce and a generous sprinkling of toasted walnuts.

Position a rack in the middle of the oven and preheat to 350°F. Lightly butter a 9-by-13-inch rectangular or oval baking dish.

Brush both sides of the brioche slices with the melted butter. Stir together ½ cup of the sugar with the cinnamon. Sprinkle both sides of the buttered brioche with the cinnamon-sugar, reserving 2 tablespoons for topping the pudding. Cut each slice into 4 squares (like big croutons), place on a baking sheet, and toast in the oven until golden brown and crisp all over, tossing occasionally, 7 to 10 minutes. Let cool completely.

continued on p. 230

In a large bowl big enough to hold the custard and the bread, whisk together the whole eggs, egg yolks, the remaining 1 cup sugar, and the vanilla. Gradually whisk in the cream and milk. Stir in the salt and mashed bananas. Add the brioche croutons and stir to coat them with the custard.

Pour the pudding mixture into the prepared dish. Cover the dish with plastic wrap and refrigerate for at least 4 hours or up to overnight to allow the bread to absorb much of the custard.

Preheat the oven to 325°F. Remove the pudding from the refrigerator and dot the top with the cold butter bits. Sprinkle with the reserved 2 tablespoons cinnamon-sugar. Cover the bread pudding with aluminum foil. Pierce a few holes in the foil to allow steam to escape. Bake for 20 minutes. Uncover the pudding and continue baking until it is puffed and golden and when a knife inserted into the center of the pudding comes out clean, 20 to 25 minutes. Let cool for 5 minutes. Cut the pudding into squares and drizzle each serving with ganache and a sprinkling of walnuts. Serve warm, with vanilla ice cream or whipped cream, if desired.

My Favorite Ganache

MAKES 1½ CUPS

- 8 ounces finely chopped semisweet chocolate
- 1 cup heavy cream
- 2 tablespoons unsalted butter
- 2 tablespoons light corn syrup

Place the chocolate in a heatproof bowl. Combine the cream, butter, and corn syrup in a saucepan. Stir over medium-high heat until the butter is melted and the corn syrup is combined with the cream. Bring to a boil. Just as the bubbles start to rise, pour the hot cream mixture over the chocolate. Let stand for 1 minute. Stir until smooth and creamy.

ALL-GROWN-UP S'MORES

MAKES 15 S'MORES

FOR THE GRAHAM CRACKER CRUST
- 3 cups crushed graham cracker crumbs
- ½ cup (1 stick) unsalted butter, melted
- 1 tablespoon granulated sugar

FOR THE CHOCOLATE FILLING
- 8 large egg yolks
- 1½ cups confectioners' sugar, sifted
- 2 tablespoons Cognac or brandy
- 2 tablespoons white crème de cacao
- 2 tablespoons Kahlúa
- 1 teaspoon pure vanilla extract
- ⅛ teaspoon salt
- 1 cup (2 sticks) unsalted butter
- 2 tablespoons Dutch-processed cocoa powder
- 12 ounces semisweet or bittersweet chocolate, finely chopped
- 1½ cups heavy cream, whipped to soft peaks

FOR THE MARSHMALLOW FLUFF MERINGUE
- 3 large egg whites
- Pinch of salt
- Pinch of cream of tartar
- ¼ teaspoon pure vanilla extract
- 1 cup Marshmallow Fluff

Topped with big loopy swirls of Marshmallow Fluff meringue burnished to a golden bronze, this S'more may be all grown up, but it still knows how to have a good time. A sweet, crumbly graham cracker crust is topped with a dense, very adult, very rich, and very boozy chocolate cream. The combination of liqueurs here is by no means written in stone: dark rum, Grand Marnier, bourbon—just pick two or three complementary flavors as you like and substitute an equal amount for what I have suggested here.

Preheat the oven to 350°F.

TO MAKE THE CRUST Combine the graham cracker crumbs with the melted butter and granulated sugar until well combined. Press into the bottom of a 9-by-13-inch metal baking pan. Bake the crust until it starts to brown and become crisp, about 10 minutes. Transfer to a wire rack and let cool completely.

TO MAKE THE FILLING Using an electric mixer, beat the egg yolks and confectioners' sugar together in a large bowl until they are thick and the color of butter. Beat in the Cognac, crème de cacao, Kahlúa, vanilla, and salt.

Melt the butter in a medium saucepan over low heat and whisk in the cocoa powder until smooth. Remove the pan from the heat, add the chocolate, and stir until the chocolate is melted and the mixture is smooth. Let cool slightly, then gradually beat into the egg mixture.

continued on p. 232

STICKY, CHEWY, MESSY, GOOEY

JILL O'CONNOR

Fold the softly beaten heavy cream into the chocolate mixture just until combined. Spoon the chocolate cream over the graham cracker crust, smoothing it evenly with a spatula. Cover the pan with plastic wrap and refrigerate until very firm, at least 4 hours or up to overnight.

WHEN READY TO SERVE, MAKE THE MERINGUE Using an electric mixer set at low speed, beat the egg whites until foamy. Add the salt and cream of tartar and beat at medium speed until soft peaks form. Beat in the vanilla. Add the Marshmallow Fluff to the egg whites a little at a time, beating constantly until stiff peaks form.

Carefully cut the S'mores into 15 large squares. Place each S'more on a dessert plate. Top each with ½ cup of the meringue in a large dollop. Use a small kitchen torch to carefully burnish the meringue until tipped with golden brown. Serve immediately.

ALL-GROWN-UP S'MORES

QUICKY STICKY BISCUITS

MAKES ABOUT 12 BIG BISCUITS

FOR THE STICKY PECAN SAUCE
- 1 cup firmly packed light brown sugar
- ½ cup dark corn syrup
- ¾ cup (1½ sticks) unsalted butter
- 1½ cups chopped pecans or walnuts, toasted

FOR THE BISCUITS
- 4 cups bleached all-purpose flour
- 2 tablespoons baking powder
- ½ teaspoon baking soda
- 1½ teaspoons salt
- 1 cup (2 sticks) very cold or frozen unsalted butter, cut into 16 pieces
- 1½ to 2 cups cold buttermilk

FOR THE TOPPING
- ½ cup granulated sugar
- 1 teaspoon ground cinnamon
- 1 stick (4 ounces) unsalted butter, melted

When I was seven years old, my mother enrolled me in my first cooking class. I loved it, and learned how to make cinnamon rolls by dipping refrigerator biscuits in melted butter and rolling them in cinnamon-sugar and walnuts before baking. Delicious! My family gobbled them up and the compliments for my cooking made me beam. Those cinnamon biscuits became a Christmas breakfast tradition for many years. I've upgraded them here with homemade Southern biscuits sprinkled with cinnamon-sugar and baked atop a sticky, gooey pecan syrup. Simple, sweet, and easy, they are a perfect grown-up version of my childhood specialty.

Position a rack in the middle of the oven and preheat to 425°F. Grease a 9-by-13-inch pan with softened butter or spray with nonstick cooking spray.

TO MAKE THE SAUCE Combine the brown sugar, corn syrup, and butter. Melt over low heat. When the butter is melted, increase the heat to high and bring to a gentle boil. Cook, uncovered, until the mixture thickens, 3 to 5 minutes. Stir in the chopped nuts. Pour the mixture into the prepared pan and spread evenly. Set aside.

TO MAKE THE BISCUITS In a large bowl, sift together twice the flour, baking powder, baking soda, and salt. Cut the butter into the flour mixture using a pastry cutter. Blend until most of the mixture looks like coarse crumbs, with some of the bits of butter the size of small peas.

Make a shallow well in the center of the flour mixture and pour in 1½ cups of the cold buttermilk. Use a fork to blend the buttermilk into the flour to create a soft dough. If the dough seems too dry as you are stirring it, add the remaining ½ cup buttermilk. Turn the dough out onto a lightly floured work surface and knead a few times to make sure it comes together. Pat the dough into a ¾-inch-thick rectangle. Use a sharp chef's knife to cut the dough into 12 square biscuits.

continued on p. 236

STICKY, CHEWY, MESSY, GOOEY

JILL O'CONNOR

EDITOR'S NOTE
Place the baking pan on a large baking sheet or line the oven floor with foil before baking these biscuits, as the sticky topping may bubble over.

TO MAKE THE TOPPING In a small bowl, stir together the granulated sugar and cinnamon. Brush the tops of the biscuits with some of the melted butter and sprinkle with some of the cinnamon-sugar. Place the biscuits, evenly spaced, cinnamon-sugar-side down, into the pecan syrup–lined pan. Brush the tops (once the bottoms) of the biscuits with more melted butter and sprinkle with a little more cinnamon-sugar.

Bake the biscuits until golden brown and puffy, and the sticky pecan sauce is bubbling around them, 15 to 17 minutes. Cool slightly, then place a large serving platter over the top of the pan and invert it. Remove the pan and allow the pecan sauce to fall around the biscuits. Use a small spatula to scrape any residual syrup from the pan onto the biscuits. Serve immediately.

best of the best exclusive

COCONUT SHORTBREAD COOKIES

MAKES 2 DOZEN COOKIES

> 2 sticks unsalted butter, at
>   room temperature
> 1 cup confectioners' sugar, sifted
> 2 teaspoons pure vanilla extract
> 2¼ cups all-purpose flour
> 1 cup sweetened shredded coconut
> ½ teaspoon salt

EDITOR'S NOTE
These shortbreads get better
over time as the coconut
softens and the flavor develops.
They're sturdy, which makes
them ideal for mailing or including
in holiday gift tins.

1. In a standing electric mixer, beat the butter with the confectioners' sugar at medium speed until pale, about 2 minutes. Add the vanilla and beat until incorporated. At low speed, beat in the flour, coconut and salt until the flour is just incorporated, about 30 seconds. Transfer the dough to a work surface and roll it into a 2-inch-wide log. Wrap the log in plastic and refrigerate until firm, about 1 hour.

2. Preheat the oven to 325°F. Line 2 baking sheets with parchment paper. Cut the log into ½-inch-thick slices and arrange them on the baking sheets at least 1 inch apart. Bake the cookies for 30 minutes, rotating the pans halfway through, until light golden around the edges and on the bottoms. Let cool for 5 minutes, then transfer the cookies to a rack to cool completely.

MAKE AHEAD The dough can be refrigerated for up to 1 week. The baked cookies can be stored in an airtight container for up to 5 days.

CHOCOLATE CHOCOLATE
STREUSEL SQUARES, P. 240

GREAT COFFEE CAKES, STICKY BUNS, MUFFINS & MORE

CAROLE WALTER

PUBLISHED BY CLARKSON POTTER, $35

This is a baking book for people who crave something sweet to eat all day long, starting with cherry honey scones sprinkled with sugar or streusel-topped sweet potato muffins for breakfast. Carole Walter takes appealingly old-fashioned recipes (which she describes as "homey" and "from yesteryear") and updates them by making them easier and faster, offering make-ahead tips wherever she can. A respected baking teacher, Walter instructs the home baker well here, with meticulous recipes labeled according to level of difficulty. She wants her readers to succeed, and anyone following her clear directions will.

featured recipes Chocolate Chocolate Streusel Squares; Powdered Sugar Pound Cake; Country Cherry Honey Scones

best of the best exclusive Nutty Banana Bread

CHOCOLATE CHOCOLATE STREUSEL SQUARES

**MAKES ONE 9 X 13 X 2-INCH CAKE,
2 DOZEN 2-INCH SERVINGS**

- 1 recipe Chocolate Streusel (recipe follows)
- 1¼ cups sifted all-purpose flour, spooned in and leveled
- ¼ cup strained Dutch-process cocoa powder
- ¾ teaspoon baking powder
- ¼ teaspoon salt
- 3 ounces unsweetened chocolate, coarsely chopped
- 6 tablespoons (¾ stick) unsalted butter
- 2 tablespoons canola or vegetable oil
- 2 large eggs
- ⅔ cup granulated sugar
- ⅓ cup (lightly packed) *very fresh* dark brown sugar
- 1 teaspoon pure vanilla extract
- ¾ cup sour cream

FINISHING
- ⅓ cup mini chocolate chips
- ½ cup medium-chopped walnuts

AT A GLANCE
PAN: 9 x 13 x 2-inch baking pan
PAN PREP: Butter generously
OVEN TEMP: 350°F
BAKING TIME: 30 to 35 minutes
DIFFICULTY: 🥄

This chocolate-packed coffee cake is a chocoholic's dream. Rich sour cream pairs with cocoa powder and unsweetened chocolate to make a cake with a tender, melt-in-your-mouth crumb. In keeping with the chocolate theme, I top the batter with buttery chocolate streusel and then add mini chocolate chips and chopped walnuts for a bit of pizzazz.

1. Prepare the Chocolate Streusel. Set aside.

2. Position the rack in the middle of the oven. Heat the oven to 350°F. Generously butter a 9 x 13 x 2-inch pan and set aside.

3. In a medium bowl, thoroughly whisk together the flour, cocoa powder, baking powder, and salt. Set aside.

4. Place the chocolate, butter, and oil in a medium, heatproof bowl and set over a pot of simmering water. (The bottom of the bowl should not touch the water.) Heat until the chocolate is melted, stirring occasionally. Keep warm.

5. Place the eggs in the bowl of an electric mixer fitted with the whip attachment. Beat on medium-high speed for 2 minutes. Add the granulated sugar, then the dark brown sugar, 1 to 2 tablespoons at a time, taking 2 minutes for each. Add the vanilla and beat for 1 minute longer. The mixture should be thick.

6. Reduce the speed to medium and add the warm chocolate mixture, mixing for 2 minutes to blend. Scrape down the side of the bowl as needed.

7. Reduce the mixer speed to low. Add the dry ingredients alternately with the sour cream, dividing the flour mixture into three parts and the sour cream into two parts, beginning and ending with the flour. Scrape down the side of the bowl.

8. Spread the batter evenly into the prepared pan. Take a handful of the streusel mixture and squeeze gently to form a large clump. Then break the clump apart, and sprinkle the crumbs onto the batter. Repeat until all of the streusel mixture has been used. *Gently* press the crumbs onto the top of the batter, sprinkle with the mini chips and walnuts, and press *gently* again.

9. Bake for 30 to 35 minutes. The cake is done when a toothpick inserted in the center comes out clean and the sides begin to pull away from the pan.

10. Remove the cake from the oven and let stand on a cake rack until cool. When ready to serve, cut into 2-inch squares.

STORAGE Store in the pan, well wrapped with aluminum foil, for up to 5 days. This cake may be frozen.

continued on p. 242

MAKES ENOUGH FOR ONE 9-INCH
ROUND OR 9 X 13 X 2-INCH COFFEE
CAKE, OR 12 TO 14 MUFFINS

6 to 7 tablespoons unsalted butter
  1 cup all-purpose flour, spooned in
     and leveled
  ¼ cup granulated sugar
  ¼ cup (lightly packed) *very fresh*
     dark brown sugar
  2 tablespoons strained Dutch-process
     cocoa powder
  ¼ teaspoon baking powder
  ¼ teaspoon salt
  ¼ teaspoon ground cinnamon

Chocolate Streusel

1. Place the butter in a 2-quart heavy-bottomed saucepan and heat until almost melted; remove from the heat and *cool until tepid*. Whisk together the flour, sugars, cocoa powder, baking powder, salt, and cinnamon. Set aside.

2. Add the dry ingredients, tossing with a fork until crumbs are formed. Gently squeeze the mixture with your hand to form larger lumps, then break them apart with your fingertips. Before using, let the streusel stand for 10 to 15 minutes.

POWDERED SUGAR POUND CAKE

**MAKES ONE 10-INCH CAKE,
16 TO 20 SERVINGS**

- 4 cups sifted cake flour, spooned in and leveled
- 2 teaspoons baking powder
- ½ teaspoon salt
- 6 large eggs
- 1½ cups (3 sticks) unsalted butter, slightly firm
- ¼ cup canola or vegetable oil
- 3½ cups strained powdered sugar, spooned in and leveled, plus extra for dusting
- 2 teaspoons pure vanilla extract
- ⅛ teaspoon lemon oil (see Editor's Note on p. 244)

AT A GLANCE

PAN: 10-inch angel food cake pan
PAN PREP: Butter generously/line with parchment/butter
OVEN TEMP: 325°F
BAKING TIME: 1 hour, 20 to 25 minutes
DIFFICULTY: ♨

If you are looking for a really terrific pound cake, you can stop here. Kept in my recipe box for years, this pound cake recipe was inspired by Nell Slagle, a dear friend from Fort Worth, Texas. Nell was a marvelous baker, and any recipe she ever recommended was always special.

The cake is made with powdered sugar, which gives it an extremely velvety texture. In Nell's day, cakes were sweeter, but I took the liberty of reducing some of the sugar. I also replaced a small amount of the butter with canola oil, which gives the cake added moistness. Be sure to drizzle in the oil slowly to retain the emulsion of the butter, and also follow the directions for adding the sugar slowly. This little extra touch will be well worth the effort. With one bite of this pound cake, I'm sure you will love it as much as I do.

1. Position the rack in the lower third of the oven. Heat the oven to 325°F. Generously butter a 10-inch angel food cake pan, line the bottom with baking parchment, then butter the parchment. Set aside.

continued on p. 244

2. In a large bowl, thoroughly whisk together the flour, baking powder, and salt. Set aside.

3. Place the eggs in a medium bowl and whisk until well blended. Set aside.

4. Cut the butter into 1-inch pieces and place in the bowl of an electric mixer fitted with the paddle attachment. Mix on medium speed until smooth and lightened in color, about 2 minutes. Slowly drizzle in the canola oil, taking about 1 minute, then beat for 2 minutes longer. Scrape down the side of the bowl.

5. Reduce the mixer speed to medium-low. *If your mixer has a splatter shield attachment, now is a good time to use it.* Add the powdered sugar, 2 to 3 tablespoons at a time, taking 8 to 10 minutes. Gradually add ½ cup of the eggs and beat for 2 minutes longer, scraping down the side of the bowl as needed. Blend in the vanilla and lemon oil.

6. Add the flour mixture alternately with the remaining eggs, dividing the flour into four parts and the eggs into three parts, beginning and ending with the flour, mixing until well blended after each addition. Scrape down the side of the bowl as needed.

7. Empty the batter into the prepared pan and smooth the top with the back of a large soupspoon. Bake for 1 hour and 20 to 25 minutes. The cake is done when the top is golden brown and firm to the touch, and a wooden skewer inserted deeply in the center comes out clean.

8. Remove the cake from the oven and let stand on a cooling rack for 25 to 30 minutes. Holding the tube, lift the cake from the outer ring and place it on the cooling rack. Let stand for another 20 to 30 minutes. Cover the cake with a cooling rack, invert, and carefully lift off the tube section of the pan and the parchment paper. Cover with another rack and turn the cake top side up to finish cooling. Dust with powdered sugar before serving.

STORAGE Store under a glass cake dome or tightly covered with plastic wrap for up to 5 days. This cake may be frozen.

COUNTRY CHERRY HONEY SCONES

MAKES 12 SCONES

- 2½ cups all-purpose flour, spooned in and leveled, plus additional for kneading and rolling
- 2 tablespoons *very fresh* light brown sugar
- 1 tablespoon baking powder
- ½ teaspoon salt
- ¼ teaspoon baking soda
- 1 teaspoon freshly grated navel orange zest
- ½ cup (1 stick) unsalted butter, cold
- ½ cup (about 2½ ounces) dried cherries (not organic), plumped and coarsely chopped (see Editor's Note on p. 248)
- 1 large egg
- ¼ cup honey
- ½ cup half-and-half
- 1 large egg lightly beaten with 1 teaspoon water, for egg wash
- 1 tablespoon sparkling sugar

AT A GLANCE
PAN: Large cookie sheet
PAN PREP: Butter
OVEN TEMP: 400°F
BAKING TIME: 14 to 16 minutes
DIFFICULTY: 🥄

If you want to make a pretty scone, this is the recipe to choose. The dough is flavored with honey and orange zest, and has chopped dried cherries throughout. When you chop the cherries, make sure they are free of pits. The scones are cut into triangles and the tops are trimmed with sparkling sugar. If you have a long basket, these are beautiful served with the tips of the triangles angled in different directions.

1. Position the rack in the middle of the oven. Heat the oven to 400°F. Butter a large cookie sheet and set aside.

2. In a large bowl, thoroughly whisk together the flour, brown sugar, baking powder, salt, and baking soda. Add the orange zest and work it into the dry ingredients with your hands.

3. Shave the butter into ⅛-inch slices using a dough scraper or sharp knife. Add the butter to the dry ingredients, rubbing it between your fingertips until the mixture resembles coarse meal. It's okay if some larger flakes of butter are visible. Add the cherries and toss to coat with the crumbs.

4. In a small bowl, combine the egg, honey, and half-and-half. Make a well in the center of the dry ingredients and add the liquid. Using a rubber spatula, draw the crumbs into the center, working your way around the side of the bowl until a soft dough is formed. With floured hands, knead the dough gently five or six times to form a "skin." Divide the dough in half and form a skin on the cut side, and set aside.

continued on p. 248

To plump the dried cherries called for here, place them in a heatproof bowl with boiling water to cover and let stand until soft; this can take up to 20 minutes, depending on how hard the cherries are to begin with. Drain well and spread on paper towels to dry.

5. Lay a pastry cloth on a pastry board or other flat surface and fit a rolling pin with a pastry sleeve. Rub about 2 tablespoons of flour into the pastry cloth and sleeve.

6. Place 1 piece of dough on the cloth and, with floured hands, turn the dough two or three times to coat it with the flour. Pat the dough into a disk, then roll it into a 7-inch circle about ½ inch thick. Cut into six wedges using a dough scraper or sharp knife. Place on the prepared cookie sheet. Repeat with the remaining dough.

7. Brush with the egg wash and sprinkle each scone with ¼ teaspoon sparkling sugar. Bake for 14 to 16 minutes, or until lightly browned. Remove from the oven and cool slightly on the cookie sheet before loosening with a thin-bladed metal spatula. Serve warm. If baking ahead, reheat the scones in a 300°F oven.

STORAGE Store in an airtight plastic bag for up to 3 days. These scones may be frozen.

best of the best exclusive
NUTTY BANANA BREAD

MAKES ONE 9-BY-5-INCH LOAF

- ¾ cup pecan halves
- 1½ cups all-purpose flour
- 1 teaspoon baking powder
- 1 teaspoon ground cinnamon
- ½ teaspoon freshly grated nutmeg
- ½ teaspoon salt
- ¼ teaspoon baking soda
- 2 large, very ripe bananas, mashed
- ¼ cup sour cream
- 1 teaspoon fresh lemon juice
- 1 teaspoon pure vanilla extract
- 2 large eggs
- ¾ cup sugar
- 4 tablespoons unsalted butter, melted
- ¼ cup canola oil

1. Preheat the oven to 350°F. Spray a 9-by-5-inch loaf pan with vegetable oil spray. Spread the pecans in a pie plate and toast for 8 minutes, until light golden and fragrant. Let the pecans cool, then coarsely chop them.

2. In a medium bowl, whisk the flour with the baking powder, cinnamon, nutmeg, salt and baking soda. In a small bowl, stir the mashed bananas with the sour cream, lemon juice and vanilla.

3. In a large bowl, using an electric mixer, beat the eggs at medium-high speed for 1 minute. With the mixer on, gradually add the sugar, taking about 2 minutes. Once the sugar is incorporated, beat until the mixture is pale and thick, about 1 minute. At medium speed, gradually beat in the butter and oil until fully incorporated. Add the banana mixture and beat until combined, about 30 seconds. At low speed, beat in the flour mixture in 2 additions until just incorporated. Using a rubber spatula, fold in the pecans.

4. Scrape the batter into the prepared loaf pan and bake in the lower third of the oven for 1 hour and 15 minutes, or until the top is golden brown and a toothpick inserted in the center comes out clean. Let the loaf cool in the pan for 10 minutes before turning it out onto a rack to cool completely.

MAKE AHEAD The banana bread can be wrapped in plastic and kept at room temperature for up to 3 days.

WELSH GRIDDLE CAKES, P. 252

A BAKER'S ODYSSEY

GREG PATENT

PUBLISHED BY JOHN WILEY & SONS, INC., $34.95

Greg Patent, who immigrated to the United States from China as a child with his Russian father and Iraqi mother, is deeply curious about how foreigners assimilate. In *A Baker's Odyssey,* he visits the American kitchens of home bakers from around the world—Lebanon, Norway, Australia—to see how they've adapted their recipes to the ingredients and equipment available here. The stories behind savory and sweet recipes like Cheese & Potato Pierogi and Welsh Griddle Cakes come together to create a fascinating and useful book for anyone intrigued by the way recipes reflect culture and evolve over time.

featured recipes Welsh Griddle Cakes; Norwegian Walnut Butter Balls; Lamingtons; Swedish Almond Jam Strips

best of the best exclusive Chocolate–Grand Marnier Cream Cake

WELSH GRIDDLE CAKES

MAKES 20 TO 24 TEA CAKES

- 4 cups cake flour
- 2 teaspoons baking powder
- ¼ teaspoon salt
- 8 tablespoons (1 stick) cold unsalted butter plus ½ cup cold lard, cut into tablespoon-sized pieces, or ½ pound (2 sticks) cold unsalted butter, cut into tablespoon-sized pieces (see headnote)
- ¾ cup granulated sugar, plus extra for sprinkling
- ½ teaspoon freshly grated nutmeg
- ¼ teaspoon ground allspice
- 1 cup golden raisins or currants, or a mixture
- Finely grated zest of 1 large lemon
- 1 large egg
- 3 tablespoons fresh lemon juice
- 1 tablespoon whole milk, plus more if needed
- All-purpose flour for rolling

These lemon-flavored tea cakes, made with golden raisins or currants, have a deliciously crumbly texture and melt in your mouth. Tottie Parmeter, who grew up in Cardiff, learned how to make them from her mother, who often would serve the cakes warm with afternoon tea. "I always looked forward to these cakes, because my mother had such a deft hand with them," she says. "And the smell of lemon, wafting up from the griddle, just made my mouth water." Tottie's mother used a combination of lard and butter. The lard contributes its own special flavor and makes the cakes especially tender. Use homemade lard or order a top-quality lard by mail. Or, if you wish, substitute butter for the lard.

This recipe dates back to the eighteenth century or earlier. In Wales, the cakes were traditionally cooked on a bakestone, a heavy cast-iron sheet that was set on coals in the fireplace. Today most bakers use an electric griddle. The dough has barely enough liquid to hold it together, which accounts for the cakes' sublime texture.

These griddle cakes are quick and easy to make. They cook in just a few minutes and are delicious with steaming-hot tea.

TO MAKE THE DOUGH BY HAND Put the flour, baking powder, and salt in a large bowl. Add the butter and lard, if using, and cut into the flour with a pastry blender or two knives until the fat particles are about the size of small peas. Reach into the bowl with both hands and rub the dry ingredients rapidly between your fingers until the consistency is like coarse sand. For the best texture, the fat must be in very small pieces. Stir in the sugar, spices, raisins or currants, and lemon zest.

TO MAKE THE DOUGH USING A FOOD PROCESSOR In a large bowl stir together the flour, baking powder, and salt. Insert the metal blade into the food processor, add about two-thirds of the dry ingredients to the work bowl, and scatter the fat on top. Pulse 5 or 6 times, then process continuously for about 10 seconds. Rub a little of the dry ingredients rapidly between your fingertips; the mixture should feel like fine meal. If necessary, process a few seconds longer. Add the contents of the work bowl to the flour in the mixing bowl and mix well. Stir in the sugar, spices, raisins or currants, and lemon zest. (From here on, follow the directions for the hand method.)

continued on p. 254

TO MAKE THE DOUGH USING A STAND MIXER Put the flour, baking powder, salt, and fat into the mixer bowl and attach the flat beater. Beat on low speed for 2 to 3 minutes, or until the mixture has the consistency of fine meal. Rub a little between your fingertips to make sure. Add the sugar, spices, raisins or currants, and lemon zest and mix on low speed for 30 seconds.

In a small bowl, lightly beat the egg with a fork. Beat in the lemon juice and milk.

TO ADD THE LIQUID BY HAND Scrape the liquid over the dry ingredients and begin stirring it in with the fork. Keep stirring and tossing until the dough forms medium to large clumps. It will seem to be quite dry. Reach into the bowl with both hands and, working quickly so as not to soften the fat, squeeze the dough together to form one mass that holds together. If the dough won't hold together, sprinkle on droplets of additional milk and squeeze again. The key to the success of this recipe is to keep the liquid to a minimum.

TO ADD THE LIQUID USING THE MIXER Scrape the liquid into the mixer bowl and mix on low speed just until the dough masses onto the beater.

EDITOR'S NOTE

As the recipe points out, the dough should be dry, but we found that it needed up to 3 tablespoons of additional milk to come together.

To shape the griddle cakes, lightly flour your work surface, place the dough on it, and roll the dough about to coat it lightly with flour. Flatten the dough a bit and roll it out until it is about ⅓ inch thick. Don't make it thicker, or the cakes will have to cook longer and they may brown too much. Stamp out circles with a sharp 2½-inch round cutter. Set the cakes on a baking sheet lined with plastic wrap. Gather the dough scraps, reroll, and cut out more cakes. Use all the dough; you may have to shape the last cake or two by hand.

Preheat a large electric nonstick griddle to 250° to 275°F. Add as many cakes as will fit comfortably, spacing them about 2 inches apart. Cook for 5 to 6 minutes, until the cakes are a deep golden brown on their bottoms. Turn them over carefully with a pancake turner and cook them on the second side for 5 to 6 minutes, until completely cooked through. The tops will feel firm and the sides will have lost their softness; a toothpick inserted into a cake should come out clean. With a wide spatula, transfer the cakes to a wire cooling rack. While they are still hot, sprinkle each cake with a pinch of sugar. Continue with the remaining cakes the same way. Serve the cakes warm or at room temperature.

STORING Once cool, the cakes can be stored airtight at room temperature for 2 to 3 days.

NORWEGIAN WALNUT BUTTER BALLS

MAKES 36 COOKIES

About 3 ounces walnuts
- 8 tablespoons (1 stick) unsalted butter, at room temperature
- 2 tablespoons granulated sugar
- ¼ teaspoon salt
- 1 teaspoon pure vanilla extract
- 1 cup unbleached all-purpose flour

About 2 cups confectioners' sugar for coating

These Norwegian shortbread cookies are made with finely ground walnuts. They are small enough to pop into your mouth, and when you bite down, the cookie crumbles and shatters into tiny pieces that soon melt into a buttery deliciousness. Cookies similar to this are found in many cultures. Dorothy Crocker, a second-generation Norwegian American, learned how to make them from her grandmother Alma Ovidia Madsen. They are really easy to make, but you'll need a manual nut grinder or a hand-held Mouli grater to grind or shred the nuts. Do not use a food processor, or the nuts may turn pasty.

Grind the nuts with a nut grinder or Mouli grater, and measure 1 cup.

In a medium bowl, beat the butter with an electric mixer on medium speed until smooth and creamy, about 30 seconds. Add the sugar, salt, and vanilla and beat for 1 to 2 minutes, until smooth and fluffy. With a wooden spoon, stir in the nuts, then stir in the flour until the dough gathers into a mass. Knead the dough briefly in the bowl until it coheres, working quickly so as not to melt the butter.

Adjust an oven rack to the center position and preheat the oven to 350°F. Line a large baking sheet (18 x 12 x 1 inch) with a silicone baking pan liner or cooking parchment.

Divide the dough into 36 equal pieces. Roll each into a smooth ball, about ¾ inch in diameter, between your palms. Place the balls 1 to 2 inches apart on the prepared sheet.

Bake until the cookies are a very pale golden brown all over, 20 to 25 minutes. They will puff a bit during baking. Remove the pan from the oven.

Place the confectioners' sugar into a large plastic bag and add about half the hot cookies. Twist the top of the bag shut and gently manipulate the bag to coat the hot cookies with a generous layer of sugar. Remove the cookies from the bag with a slotted spoon and set them on wire racks to cool completely. Repeat with the remaining cookies while they are still hot.

STORING Store the cookies in airtight containers at room temperature for up to 1 week. To freeze, place the sugared cookies on a parchment- or foil-lined baking sheet and freeze until solid, then transfer to heavy-duty resealable plastic bags and freeze for up to 1 month. Thaw the cookies completely in their wrapping. Dust again with confectioners' sugar, if necessary.

LAMINGTONS

MAKES 24 INDIVIDUAL CAKES

CAKE
- 1¾ cups bleached all-purpose flour, plus more for the pan
- 2 teaspoons baking powder
- 12 tablespoons (1½ sticks) salted butter, at room temperature
- 1½ cups granulated sugar
- 1½ teaspoons pure vanilla extract
- 3 large eggs
- 1 cup whole milk

CHOCOLATE SAUCE
- 4 cups confectioners' sugar
- ½ cup unsweetened cocoa powder
- 4 tablespoons (½ stick) salted butter, melted
- ⅔ cup boiling water

3 to 4 cups shredded unsweetened coconut

Lamingtons are to Australians what chocolate cupcakes are to Americans. They are squares of yellow butter cake dipped into a chocolate sauce and coated with unsweetened coconut. Elizabeth Germaine's cooking students in Melbourne adored them, and she loved making them; she now makes Lamingtons regularly in the United States. "They're so simple, yet sophisticated in their own way, and so much fun to eat," she says. The success of a Lamington largely depends on the quality of the cake. It must be a firm-textured butter cake with a fine crumb, which is exactly what you'll get with the recipe below. For best results, it should be made a day ahead.

The dessert is named for Baroness Lamington, the wife of an early-twentieth-century political official in Australia. Lamingtons are a national favorite, sold at almost every bake sale in Australia and practically every bakery. Kids love eating them out of hand, but you can serve them at a tea party with knife and fork. A scoop of vanilla ice cream goes very well with a Lamington.

Shredded unsweetened coconut is available in many supermarkets and in health-food stores or by mail order. If you prefer, make the variation using macadamia nuts instead of coconut.

continued on p. 260

TO MAKE THE CAKE Adjust an oven rack to the lower third position and preheat the oven to 350°F. Grease a 13 x 9 x 2-inch baking pan, dust it with flour, and knock out the excess flour.

Whisk the flour and baking powder together in a medium bowl.

Beat the butter in a large bowl with an electric mixer on medium speed until smooth. Add ¼ cup of the sugar and the vanilla and beat for 30 seconds. While beating, gradually add the remaining 1¼ cups sugar. Scrape the bowl and beater, then beat for 5 minutes on medium-high speed. Add the eggs one at a time, beating well after each. On low speed, add the flour mixture in 3 additions alternately with the milk in 2 additions, beginning and ending with the dry ingredients and beating only until smooth. Scrape the batter into the prepared pan and smooth the top.

Bake for 35 to 40 minutes, until the cake is golden brown and pulls away slightly from the sides of the pan and a toothpick inserted into the center comes out clean. Cool the cake in its pan on a wire rack for 15 minutes, then cover the cake pan with a wire rack and invert the two. Remove the pan, cover the cake with another rack, and invert the cake again to cool completely right side up.

Drape the cake loosely with a kitchen towel and leave at room temperature overnight.

With a sharp serrated knife, trim the crusts from the sides of the cake. Cut the cake into 24 squares.

TO MAKE THE CHOCOLATE SAUCE In a medium metal bowl whisk together the confectioners' sugar, cocoa, butter, and boiling water until smooth. Set the bowl into a pan of very hot water to keep the sauce fluid. Spread the coconut in a shallow dish or pie plate. Drop a piece of cake into the chocolate sauce and use two long-tined forks to turn the cake quickly in the sauce to coat all surfaces. Lift the cake out of the sauce, letting excess sauce drip back into the bowl, and transfer the cake to the bowl of coconut. Use your fingers to sprinkle the cake with coconut, rolling it around to coat all surfaces well. Remove the cake from the coconut and set it on a wire cooling rack. Repeat with the remaining cake. Leave the cakes on the wire racks to dry for 1 to 2 hours before serving.

STORING Lamingtons keep well for 3 to 4 days, stored in an airtight container at room temperature.

VARIATION For utter extravagance, and for Lamingtons with a completely different quality, you can substitute about 1 pound salted or unsalted macadamia nuts (which originated in Australia), finely chopped, for the coconut.

SWEDISH ALMOND JAM STRIPS

MAKES ABOUT 48 COOKIES

DOUGH

¾ cup unblanched almonds

15 tablespoons unsalted butter, at room temperature

¼ cup plus 3 tablespoons granulated sugar

¼ teaspoon salt

1⅔ cups unbleached all-purpose flour (spooned into the cups and leveled)

¾ to 1 cup seedless raspberry jam

GLAZE

1 cup confectioners' sugar

½ teaspoon pure vanilla extract

1 tablespoon boiling water, plus more if needed

These classic buttery Swedish cookies, called syltängder med mandel, *are as addictive as potato chips. The tender yet crunchy cookies filled with tangy sweet raspberry jam are an irresistible taste and texture combination. Helena Hoas, who emigrated from Sweden more than twenty years ago, makes these regularly. She shapes the dough lovingly, as though she were dressing a baby. She makes the troughs to contain the jam by running a fingertip slowly up and down the lengths of dough, and she fills them with just the right amount of jam. "You have to be careful not to put in too much," she says, "or the jam will overflow and the cookies won't be as pretty as they should be." The cookies are best when very fresh. "They are very easy to make," Helena says. "I just make sure there'll be lots of people around to eat them all."*

Adjust an oven rack to the center position and preheat the oven to 350°F. Line a large (17 x 14-inch) cookie sheet with a silicone baking pan liner or cooking parchment.

TO MAKE THE DOUGH Grind the almonds to a fine powder using a nut grinder. Lacking that, process them to a powder with 3 tablespoons of the sugar in a food processor fitted with the metal blade (beat the remaining sugar into the butter). Be careful not to overprocess them, or they may turn pasty.

In a medium bowl, beat the butter with an electric mixer on medium speed until smooth, about 1 minute. Add the sugar and salt and beat for 2 to 3 minutes, until fluffy. Scrape the bowl. On low speed, beat in the almonds. Gradually beat in the flour, beating only until incorporated.

Turn the dough out onto a lightly floured surface and shape it into a thick disk. Divide the dough into 4 portions, and roll each

piece into a log about 12 inches long and 1 inch wide. Put the logs crosswise onto the prepared sheet, leaving about 3 inches of space between them.

Leaving the ends of the rolls intact, make a shallow depression down the length of each roll about ½ inch wide and ½ inch deep. You can use a fingertip or the handle of a wooden spoon, and you may need to go up and down the length of each roll 2 or 3 times. Don't make the trough too deep, or the rolls may crack. Use a small spoon to fill the depressions with the jam. The jam should be only a tiny bit higher than the rims of the troughs; if you use too much, it will run down the sides of the rolls during baking.

Bake for about 25 minutes, until the rolls are a light golden brown. Rotate the sheet front to back once during baking to ensure even browning. Remove the pan from the oven and set it on a wire cooling rack.

AS SOON AS THE ROLLS COME OUT OF THE OVEN, MAKE THE GLAZE Whisk the confectioners' sugar, vanilla, and boiling water together in a small bowl. Gradually add a little more water if necessary to make a glaze the consistency of heavy cream. Spoon the icing over the jam, not the sides of the rolls. You may not need to use all the glaze. Cool the rolls for 5 minutes.

Using a large cookie sheet as a spatula, transfer the rolls to a cutting surface. Use a sharp heavy knife to cut the hot rolls at an angle into cookies about 1¼ inches wide. Cool completely on wire racks.

STORING Stored airtight at room temperature, the cookies will remain fresh for a few days.

best of the best exclusive

CHOCOLATE–GRAND MARNIER CREAM CAKE

SERVES 8 TO 10

CAKE

1¼ cups all-purpose flour, sifted
1 teaspoon cream of tartar
1 teaspoon baking soda
2 tablespoons distilled white vinegar
2 tablespoons cold water
6 large eggs, at room temperature, separated
1½ cups sugar
1½ tablespoons finely grated orange zest
3 tablespoons fresh orange juice
1 teaspoon pure orange extract

CHOCOLATE–GRAND MARNIER CREAM

8 ounces bittersweet chocolate
2 cups heavy cream, at room temperature
2 tablespoons Grand Marnier

EDITOR'S NOTE

To make the chocolate–Grand Marnier cream, it's essential that both the cream and the melted chocolate are at room temperature. If not, you'll end up with speckles of hardened chocolate in the cream—still delicious, but not as luxuriously smooth.

1. MAKE THE CAKE Preheat the oven to 350°F. Butter and flour two 9-inch cake pans. In a medium bowl, whisk the flour with the cream of tartar and baking soda. In a small bowl, combine the vinegar with the cold water.

2. In a food processor, blend the egg whites until thickened, about 10 seconds. With the machine on, gradually pour the vinegar mixture through the feed tube and process until the egg whites are whipped, about 1 minute. Transfer the whites to a large bowl. Add the sugar and orange zest to the food processor and process until the zest is minced, about 30 seconds. Add the egg yolks, orange juice and orange extract and process until the mixture is smooth and thick, scraping down the side of the bowl halfway through, about 1 minute. Spoon the flour mixture in a ring around the egg yolk mixture, then spoon the whipped egg whites in a ring on top of the flour. Pulse twice, for 1 second each time, until almost fully incorporated. Scrape down the side of the bowl and pulse once more, just until the whites are fully incorporated.

3. Divide the batter between the prepared pans and bake for 35 minutes, until the cakes are deep golden and start to come away from the sides of the pans. Let the cakes cool in the pans for 5 minutes, then run a small, sharp knife around the edges of the cakes. Invert the cakes onto racks and let cool completely.

4. MAKE THE CHOCOLATE–GRAND MARNIER CREAM In a medium bowl set over a medium saucepan of simmering water, melt the chocolate. Remove from the heat and let stand until cooled to room temperature. In a large bowl, whip the cream with the Grand Marnier until firm. Fold 1 cup of the whipped cream into the cooled chocolate, then fold the chocolate into the remaining whipped cream until no streaks remain.

5. Using a serrated knife, split the cakes in half horizontally. Place the top half of one of the cakes cut side up on a cake platter. Spread the cake with a ¼-inch-thick layer of the chocolate cream. Top with the bottom half of the cake, cut side down. Repeat with another 2 layers of the chocolate cream and the remaining cake layers to make a 4-layer cake. Spread the remaining chocolate cream over the top and side of the cake. Refrigerate the cake for 2 hours, until the chocolate cream is set. Using a serrated knife, cut the cake into wedges and serve.

MAKE AHEAD The frosted cake can be refrigerated for up to 1 day. Bring to room temperature before serving.

ITALIAN CHOCOLATE-
ALMOND TORTE, P. 268

PURE DESSERT

ALICE MEDRICH

PUBLISHED BY ARTISAN, $35

Most dessert books celebrate sugar, flour and butter; Alice Medrich's champions whole grains, olive oil, chestnut flour, cheese and other local, artisanal, organic ingredients presented in the most unadorned, "pure" way (there are no glazes, fillings or frostings here). Medrich, who opened her pioneering Cocolat bakery in Berkeley in the seventies and who has written several award-winning cookbooks, is obsessive about her recipe writing and testing, and it shows. These desserts aren't supersweet, which makes them amazingly versatile. Her Dried Fruit & Nut Cake, for instance, loaded with dried pears and plums, dates and walnuts, is as delicious with a wedge of Camembert as a cup of tea.

featured recipes Italian Chocolate-Almond Torte; Very Tangy Lime or Lemon Bars; Gianduja Roulade; Dried Fruit & Nut Cake

best of the best exclusive Olive Oil Cake with Saffron & Cardamom

Find more recipes by Alice Medrich at foodandwine.com/medrich.

ITALIAN CHOCOLATE-ALMOND TORTE
TORTA CIOCCOLATA

SERVES 10

EQUIPMENT: A 9-INCH SPRINGFORM PAN OR A 9 BY 3-INCH ROUND PAN WITH A REMOVABLE BOTTOM

- 1 cup (5 ounces) unblanched or blanched whole almonds
- 7 ounces good-quality unsweetened chocolate, roughly chopped
- 1 cup sugar
- ⅛ teaspoon salt
- 7 large egg whites (1 cup)
- ¼ teaspoon cream of tartar
- Powdered sugar or unsweetened cocoa powder for dusting
- Sweetened whipped cream for serving (optional)

The soul of simplicity, this jewel of a chocolate dessert was inspired by Claudia Roden's torta di mandorle e cioccolata *in her magnificent* Book of Jewish Food. *The torte is rich and quite sophisticated, yet simple to make. Lots of ground, rather than melted, unsweetened chocolate and plenty of almonds folded into egg whites (no yolks) produce a uniquely moist, rich torte with a nutty texture but without the dense heaviness you might expect.*

Position a rack in the lower third of the oven and preheat the oven to 350°F. Grease the sides of the springform pan and line the bottom with parchment paper.

Combine the almonds, chocolate, ½ cup of the sugar, and the salt in a food processor and pulse until the almonds and chocolate are very finely chopped but not completely pulverized. Set aside.

In the clean dry bowl of a stand mixer or using a hand-held mixer and a large bowl, beat the egg whites with cream of tartar until soft, moist peaks are formed when the beaters are lifted. Gradually add the remaining ½ cup sugar and continue to beat until the egg whites are stiff but not dry. Add one-third of the nut mixture to the egg whites and fold in with a large rubber spatula until nearly incorporated. Fold in half of the remaining nuts, then fold in the rest of the nuts.

Scrape the batter into the prepared pan and spread it evenly. Bake until the torte has risen and is golden brown on top and a toothpick inserted in the center of the cake comes out clean, or with a little melted chocolate, 25 to 30 minutes. Set the pan on a rack to cool for 10 minutes. Remove the sides of the pan and invert the cake onto the rack. Remove the bottom of the pan and then the parchment liner. Turn the cake right side up and cool completely. Cover or wrap tightly, and store for up to 3 days at room temperature.

To serve, transfer the cake to a serving plate. Dust with powdered sugar or cocoa, and serve slices with a dollop of whipped cream, if desired.

VERY TANGY LIME OR LEMON BARS

**MAKES 16 LARGE BARS OR
25 SMALLER BARS**

**EQUIPMENT: AN 8-INCH SQUARE
BAKING PAN**

FOR THE CRUST

8 tablespoons (1 stick) unsalted
   butter, melted
¼ cup sugar
¾ teaspoon pure vanilla extract
¼ teaspoon salt
1 cup (4.5 ounces) all-purpose flour

FOR THE TOPPING

1 cup plus 2 tablespoons sugar
3 tablespoons all-purpose flour
3 large eggs
1½ teaspoons finely grated lime or
   lemon zest, preferably from an
   organic or unsprayed fruit
½ cup strained fresh lime or lemon
   juice, preferably from an organic
   or unsprayed fruit (see Note)
Powdered sugar for dusting
   (optional)

I love lemon and lime desserts but often find them overly sweetened or their puckery-ness "tamed" with too much baking soda. (Baking soda reduces the acidity of the citrus juice.) An esteemed New England cooking magazine once pronounced my lemon bars too sour, though my cooking students and guests continue to declare them the best ever. Perhaps it's a New England versus California thing. I mention this so you know what you are getting into here: very special (and very tangy) citrus bars with a tender, crunchy crust.

Position a rack in the lower third of the oven and preheat the oven to 350°F. Line the bottom and up the sides of the baking pan with foil.

TO MAKE THE CRUST In a medium bowl, combine the melted butter with the sugar, vanilla, and salt. Add the flour and mix just until incorporated. Press the dough evenly over the bottom of the pan.

Bake for 25 to 30 minutes, or until the crust is fully baked, well browned at the edges, and golden brown in the center.

WHILE THE CRUST IS BAKING, MAKE THE TOPPING Stir together the sugar and flour in a large bowl until well mixed. Whisk in the eggs. Stir in the lemon or lime zest and juice.

When the crust is ready, turn the oven down to 300°F. Slide the rack with the pan out, and pour the filling onto the hot crust. Bake for 20 to 25 minutes longer, or until the topping no longer jiggles in the center when the pan is tapped. Set on a rack to cool completely in the pan.

EDITOR'S NOTE
When you line the baking pan
with foil, put the dull side up—food
is less likely to stick to it. Also,
be sure to leave an inch or two of
foil hanging over the edges
of the pan so that you can easily
lift the bars out after baking.

Lift up the foil liner and transfer the bars to a cutting board.
If the surface is covered with a thin layer of moist foam
(not unusual), you can blot it gently to reveal the zest. Lay
a square of paper towel on the surface and sweep your
fingers over it gently to absorb excess moisture. Remove
the paper and repeat with a fresh piece if necessary. Use a
long sharp knife to cut into sixteen 2-inch or 25 daintier
bars. Sift powdered sugar over the bars just before serving,
if desired. The bars can be stored airtight in the refrigerator
for several days or more. After 3 days, the crust softens but
the bars still taste quite good for up to a week.

NOTE Meyer lemons are less tart and more floral than
most other lemons. If you want to use them, reduce the
sugar in the topping to ½ cup plus 2 tablespoons.

GIANDUJA ROULADE

SERVES 10

**EQUIPMENT: RIMMED BAKING SHEET
OR A 12 BY 16-INCH OR 11 BY 17-INCH
JELLY-ROLL PAN**

FOR THE FILLING

6 ounces milk-chocolate-based
    gianduja, coarsely chopped, or
    5 ounces dark-chocolate gianduja
1 cup heavy cream

FOR THE CAKE

⅓ cup (1.5 ounces) hazelnuts (plus a
    few extra for testing doneness)
2 tablespoons all-purpose flour
6 ounces 70% bittersweet chocolate,
    coarsely chopped
8 tablespoons (1 stick) unsalted
    butter, cut into chunks
4 large eggs, separated
⅔ cup sugar
⅛ teaspoon salt
⅛ teaspoon cream of tartar
Cocoa powder for dusting
Powdered sugar for dusting (optional)

*A thin layer of bittersweet chocolate and toasted hazelnut
soufflé cake rolled up around chocolate hazelnut cream.
Dreamy, rich, and impressive.*

TO MAKE THE FILLING Place the gianduja in a medium bowl.
Bring the cream to a simmer and pour it over the gianduja.
Stir until the gianduja is completely melted. Cover and chill
the mixture until very cold, 4 hours or more.

TO MAKE THE CAKE Position a rack in the center of the oven
and preheat the oven to 350°F.

Spread the nuts in a baking pan or pie pan and toast until
flavorful and golden brown in the center, 10 to 15 minutes.
Cool completely, then rub off the loose skins. Line
the baking sheet or jelly-roll pan with parchment paper.

Combine the nuts with the flour in a clean food processor
(or mini processor) bowl, and pulse until the nuts are finely
ground. Set aside.

Combine the chocolate and butter in a large heatproof bowl,
set it in a wide skillet of barely simmering water, and stir
occasionally until the mixture is melted and smooth. Off the
heat, stir in the egg yolks, ⅓ cup of the sugar, and the salt.

In a clean dry mixer or other large bowl, beat the egg whites
and cream of tartar with a stand mixer on medium speed
until soft peaks form. Gradually sprinkle in the remaining
⅓ cup sugar, and continue beating at high speed until
the whites are stiff but not dry.

Use a rubber spatula to fold about one-quarter of the egg whites into the chocolate mixture. Scrape the remaining egg whites into the bowl, pour the nut mixture over them, and fold until no streaks remain.

Spread the batter evenly in the prepared pan. Bake until a toothpick inserted into the center of the cake comes out just clean, 8 to 10 minutes. Cool completely in the pan on a rack.

Sift a light dusting of cocoa over the top of the cake. Run a knife around the edges of the pan to detach the cake. Cover the cake with a sheet of foil long enough to extend over the ends of the pan. Holding the foil against the edges of the pan, invert the cake, and peel off the pan liner.

Whip the gianduja cream until it thickens and holds its shape. Spread the cream evenly over the cake (if it is so stiff it tears the cake, spread it with a warmed spatula). Starting at one short side, roll the cake, using the foil to help you. At first the cake will crack as you roll it—do not worry, the cracking will get less severe as the roulade gets fatter, and a little cracking on the finished roulade looks quite appetizing anyway. Wrap the roulade in the foil and refrigerate for at least 2 hours, or until firm.

To serve, unwrap the roulade and slide it onto a platter. Sift a little more cocoa over it, and, if desired, a little powdered sugar for contrast. Slice and serve.

DRIED FRUIT & NUT CAKE

MAKES 1 LARGE LOAF CAKE OR
2 SMALL ONES

EQUIPMENT: A 9 BY 5-INCH 8-CUP LOAF
PAN OR TWO 8 BY 4-INCH (4 CUPS)
LOAF PANS

¾ cup (3.4 ounces) all-purpose flour

¼ teaspoon baking soda

¼ teaspoon baking powder

½ teaspoon salt

¾ cup (5.25 ounces) firmly packed light or dark brown sugar or raw sugar, such as light muscovado or grated piloncillo

1 cup dried apricots, plums, pluots, pears, or peaches, or a mixture (to measure, leave apricots or similar-size fruit whole and cut larger fruit in halves or thirds)

2 cups quartered moist dates or any other favorite dried fruits

3 cups (12 ounces) walnut halves

3 large eggs

1 teaspoon pure vanilla extract

My friend Christine Blaine gave me this recipe many years ago when she was the retail director of my dessert company. Chock-full of crunchy nuts and moist dried fruit, it was especially appealing for having no artificially colored (and universally reviled) bits of candied fruit. This is an even more treasured recipe now that there are so many more dried fruits with which to create variations. (For the cake in the photograph, I used dates, dried Angelino plums, and dried pears.) Please be inventive with this fantastic recipe. Add slices to the cheese tray, or serve with after-dinner liqueurs. Or keep some in your desk for an emergency burst of energy.

Position a rack in the lower third of the oven and preheat the oven to 300°F. Spray the loaf pans with vegetable oil spray or line the bottom and sides with parchment paper.

In a large bowl, whisk the flour with the baking soda, baking powder, and salt to combine. Add the brown sugar, all the dried fruit, and the nuts and mix thoroughly with your fingers. Set aside.

continued on p. 276

PURE DESSERT

ALICE MEDRICH

This dense, fruity-nutty cake is habit-forming. It's a little bit like a sweet bread—ideal with a cup of tea, a wedge of Camembert or served for breakfast alongside tangy Greek yogurt.

In a small bowl, beat the eggs with the vanilla until light. Pour the egg mixture over the dry ingredients and mix well with a wooden spoon or your hands until all the fruits and nuts are coated with batter. Scrape into the prepared pan(s).

Bake until the top is deep golden brown and the batter clinging to the fruit seems set, about 1 hour and 10 minutes for smaller loaves, 10 to 15 minutes longer for a large loaf. Tent loosely with foil if the cake appears to be browning too much. Cool completely in the pan(s) on a rack.

When completely cool, remove the cake from the pan(s). The cake keeps, wrapped airtight in foil or plastic wrap, for several weeks at room temperature or at least 3 months in the refrigerator. It can also be frozen for at least 6 months.

To serve, cut into thin slices with a sharp heavy knife.

best of the best exclusive

OLIVE OIL CAKE WITH SAFFRON & CARDAMOM

MAKES ONE 8-INCH CAKE

Pinch of saffron threads, crumbled
½ cup whole milk
1½ cups all-purpose flour
1 teaspoon baking powder
1 cup granulated sugar
½ cup extra-virgin olive oil
1 teaspoon pure vanilla extract
¾ teaspoon ground cardamom
  (see Note)
⅛ teaspoon salt
2 large eggs
2 large egg yolks
Confectioners' sugar, for dusting

EDITOR'S NOTE

For the best flavor, use good-quality saffron sparingly: not more than a scant ⅛ teaspoon crumbled. Its flavor will intensify as the cake sits—in fact, the cake tastes best the day after it's made. If you're not a saffron fan, leave it out.

1. Preheat the oven to 350°F. Butter and flour an 8-inch round cake pan. In a small bowl, sprinkle the saffron over the milk and let stand for 15 minutes. Sift the flour and baking powder onto a large piece of parchment paper.

2. In a standing mixer fitted with a whip, beat the sugar with the olive oil, vanilla, cardamom and salt at medium-high speed until well blended. Add the eggs and egg yolks 1 at a time, beating well after each addition. Continue to beat at medium-high speed until the mixture is pale and thick, about 4 minutes. At low speed, alternately beat in the flour mixture and milk in 3 additions, scraping down the side of the bowl as necessary.

3. Scrape the batter into the prepared pan and bake for 50 minutes, until the top is golden and a cake tester inserted in the center comes out clean. Let the cake cool in the pan for 15 minutes, then invert the cake onto a rack. Turn the cake right side up and let cool completely. Dust the top of the cake with confectioners' sugar, slice into wedges and serve.

NOTE Buy the freshest ground cardamom for the best flavor. Alternatively, you can crush 12 cardamom pods and grind the seeds in a spice grinder or in a mortar.

MAKE AHEAD The cake can be wrapped in plastic and kept at room temperature for up to 2 days. Dust with confectioners' sugar before serving.

CREDITS

On the Cover
"Taboret" table by Bungalow 5, bungalow5.com.
"Bamboo/Spice" flooring from Lowes, lowes.com.

Crescent City Cooking
Unforgettable Recipes from
Susan Spicer's New Orleans
From *Crescent City Cooking* by Susan Spicer with
Paula Disbrowe. Copyright © 2007 by Susan Spicer.
Photographs by Chris Granger. Reprinted by permission
of Alfred A. Knopf, a division of Random House, Inc.

Bobby Flay's
Mesa Grill Cookbook
Explosive Flavors from the
Southwestern Kitchen
From *Bobby Flay's Mesa Grill Cookbook: Explosive Flavors
from the Southwestern Kitchen* by Bobby Flay with
Stephanie Banyas and Sally Jackson, copyright © 2007 by
Boy Meets Grill, Inc. Used by permission of Clarkson Potter/
Publishers, a division of Random House, Inc. Photographs
copyright © 2007 by Ben Fink.

Isabel's Cantina
Bold Latin Flavors from the
New California Kitchen
From *Isabel's Cantina: Bold Latin Flavors from the New
California Kitchen* by Isabel Cruz, copyright © 2007 by Isabel
Cruz. Used by permission of Clarkson Potter/Publishers,
a division of Random House, Inc. Photographs copyright
© 2007 by Gregory Bertolini.

The Young Man & the Sea
Recipes & Crispy Fish Tales from Esca
Excerpted from *The Young Man & the Sea.* Copyright © 2007
by David Pasternack and Ed Levine. Used by permission
of Artisan, a division of Workman Publishing Co., Inc.,
New York. All rights reserved. Photographs copyright
© 2007 by Christopher Hirsheimer.

The Art of Simple Food
Notes, Lessons & Recipes
from a Delicious Revolution
From *The Art of Simple Food* by Alice Waters, copyright
© 2007 by Alice Waters. Used by permission of Clarkson
Potter/Publishers, a division of Random House, Inc.

Cook with Jamie
My Guide to Making You a Better Cook
Excerpted from *Cook with Jamie* by Jamie Oliver.
Copyright © 2007 by Jamie Trevor Oliver. All rights reserved.
Published by Hyperion. Available wherever books are sold.
Photographs copyright © 2007 by David Loftus and Chris Terry.

Cristina's Tuscan Table
From *Cristina's Tuscan Table* by Cristina Ceccatelli
Cook. Text copyright © 2007 by Cristina Ceccatelli Cook.
Photographs copyright © 2007 by Kirsten Shultz.
Reprinted by permission of Gibbs Smith, Publisher.

Mediterranean Harvest
Vegetarian Recipes from the
World's Healthiest Cuisine
Reprinted from: *Mediterranean Harvest* by Martha Rose
Shulman. Copyright © 2007 by Martha Rose Shulman.
Permission granted by Rodale, Inc., Emmaus, PA 18098.
Available wherever books are sold or directly from the
publisher by calling (800) 848-4735 or visit their website
at www.rodalestore.com.

Sweet Myrtle & Bitter Honey
The Mediterranean Flavors of Sardinia
From *Sweet Myrtle & Bitter Honey* by Efisio Farris with
Jim Eber. Copyright © 2007 by GourmetSardinia Co. Food
photographs copyright © by Laurie Smith. Reprinted
by permission of Rizzoli International Publications, Inc.

Tapas
The Little Dishes of Spain
From *Tapas* by Penelope Casas. Copyright © 1985, 2007
by Penelope Casas. Photographs by Jim Smith. Reprinted by
permission of Alfred A. Knopf, a division of Random House, Inc.

Savory Baking from the Mediterranean
Focaccias, Flatbreads, Rusks, Tarts
& Other Breads
Four recipes and book cover image from *Savory Baking
from the Mediterranean* by Anissa Helou. Copyright © 2007
by Anissa Helou. Reprinted by permission of HarperCollins
Publishers. William Morrow.

The Shun Lee Cookbook
Recipes from a Chinese Restaurant Dynasty
Four recipes, four photos and book cover image from
The Shun Lee Cookbook by Michael Tong. Copyright © 2007
by Michael Tong and Elaine Louie. Reprinted by permission
of HarperCollins Publishers. William Morrow.

INDEX

INDEX

INDEX

INDEX

FOOD&WINE
BOOKS

More books from
FOOD&WINE

Annual Cookbook 2008
Over 650 recipes from the world's best cooks—
from chefs like Mario Batali and Thomas Keller to
the talented staff of the F&W Test Kitchen.

Cocktails 2008
More than 175 amazing drink and snack recipes from
America's hottest bars and restaurants, plus an indispensable
guide to cocktail basics and the country's best nightspots.

Wine Guide 2008
The most up-to-date guide, with more than 1,500
recommendations and an easy-to-use food pairing tip sheet.